THE
SCIENCE
AND ART OF
THE PENDULUM:
A Complete Course in Radiesthesia

by
Gabriele Blackburn

Published in 1983 by: IDYLWILD BOOKS
P.O. Box 246
Ojai, CA 93023

Library of Congress Catalog Card Number 83-83220
ISBN 0-9613054-1-X

Cover Design by Fred Colcer
Interior Design and Production: The Word Shop, Inc.

Manufactured in the United States of America

First Printing April 1984
Second Printing April 1985
Third Printing August 1987
Fourth Printing June 1992
Fifth Printing March 2001

A very special thank you to
Dr. Hazel Parcells,
who was my first Radiesthesia teacher
and started me on my way.

CONTENTS

LIST OF DIAGRAMS

AUTHOR'S NOTE

To Former and New Students

As many of you know, I began sharing this course material in 1977. Since then I have taught Radiesthesia seminars, as well as Healing Development and Laying-on-of-Hands seminars, in the United States, Canada, and in Europe. Everywhere I went there were students from all walks of life: professional healers, therapists and practitioners of all kinds, as well as laymen. Each student contributed to this course. Over the years I have made many additions and refinements, leading to changes in the subject material, the Work-List Pages, and the Anatomy Charts, as well as in the production of the course materials. My very sincere and warmest thanks to all of you for participating in this continual learning adventure; you have all helped to bring this course into the Light. I will always welcome your comments and any further uses of the pendulum that you may have found, so that we can all share in any new knowledge.

I want to make it very clear that I do not accept the responsibility of working with the pendulum for others, so please do not send me any inquiries concerning this. That is one of the reasons why I wrote this book; so that you can work to heal yourself: take responsibility for yourself.

I have been working with patients for over twenty years in the psychological area, having been trained by Phyllis Krystal in the reverie, or waking-dream state: a state of inner awareness.[1] I also do spiritual healing, laying-on-of-hands, and self-healing work; in other words, holistic spiritual healing.

I wish those of you who are starting anew on this wonderful adventure the very best of luck. I feel you can find a great 'friend' in the pendulum, for after all, you will be working with your own innate wisdom, which unites you to the consciousness of all mankind.

[1]Krystal, Phyllis. *Cutting the Ties that Bind.* Aura Books, Los Angeles 1983.

CHAPTER ONE

Introducing the Pendulum

The History

The art of using a pendulum is very ancient. We do not know when the practice first started, but mention is made of its use by the Hebrews, Egyptians, and ancient Chinese as early as 2000 B.C. For many years its use was confined to the priesthood and was therefore shrouded in mystery. But it also was employed in dowsing to find water, and when it was introduced into Europe the element of mystery was removed to some extent when it began to be used in dowsing for such minerals as gold, silver, and oil, as well as in the diagnosis of disease. Even today many people believe it to be something for which a special skill is required. The importance of the pendulum as a unique tool is realized only by those relative few who have studied and experimented along these lines.

How and Why the Pendulum Works

In our present society the shroud of mystery has been lifted from many subjects that once were considered mysterious. Nowadays many intelligent people are searching for ways to bridge the gap which has existed between science, religion, and occultism, and it is acknowledged that there is only a thin dividing line between physics and mysticism. The oneness of life is beginning to be recognized and it is becoming evident that universal laws govern our world at all levels. The personal consciousness which we feel as uniquely our own, is but a part of the larger collective consciousness of humanity. It would seem that the individual experiences and wisdom that each of us collects during a lifetime becomes a part of the collective consciousness. The brain cells which are being passed on to each succeeding generation through the hereditary process are encoded with this inherent information. Though not consciously remembered, the information is there as an existing potential. Each new generation has the possibility of carrying the torch of human understanding a little further.

It is this fact which makes the mastering of the pendulum so exciting, for it allows the pendulist to tune into the storehouse of the collective consciousness. In this way, information is available from an inexhaustible source and not confined to the knowledge of but one individual, no matter how well-informed he may be. In theory, the pendulist may receive verifiable information on almost any subject that has been known to other men throughout the ages. However, certain prerequisites are required. This is a precise science dealing with facts which can be verified, and as such it requires a serious approach. The answer which is sought must be useful, nonegocentric, and reasonable. The question must be a "right question" concerning factual matters; there is, for instance, no use asking the color of the hair on a tortoise!

The Psi Factor

Apparently the Psi factor or intuitive sensing enters into the matter. This bridges the usual gap between the personal and universal consciousness. We all contribute to the universal collective consciousness, which is the sum total of all human experience. The pendulist if sufficiently sensitive, is able to tune into this reservoir. In this way the pendulist can detect the radiations from objects and conditions in the human body, thereby bringing together physics and metaphysics.

Abbé Mermet

One of the first men who contributed the most to the study and technique of the pendulum was a country priest in France by the name of Abbé Mermet, who was considered to be one of the foremost dowsers for water in Europe. He studied and developed the natural sensitivity of the human organism to radiations and force-fields, and then applied his knowledge to the discovery of disease, locating missing persons, and to solving all kinds of problems. Near the end of his life he wrote down and published everything that he knew in his book, *The Principles and Practice of Radiesthesia*, a book that remains a classic in its field. Anyone interested in the technical data and theories of how and why the pendulum works is referred to this publication. Abbé Mermet's method is used in Europe but is different from the one taught in America. It bears further study, especially as applied to dowsing for water (which has many pitfalls). Abbé Mermet was highly respected both in his ministry and for the help he was able to give others through his use of the pendulum. The Vatican took great interest in his work and asked him to teach not only other priests but men of medicine as well.

In England, Dr. H. Tomlinson has done revolutionary work using radiesthesia in the field of medicine. He found the use of aluminum utensils causes the poisoning of food, and that a great many diseases are the result of such contamination.[1] His work represents an entirely new method of diagnosis and treatment which could revolutionize orthodox medicine.[2]

Edward Bach

Dr. Edward Bach, who lived from 1880-1936, was a well-known bacteriologist and researcher in London. He gave up his Harley Street practice and went to Wales to search intuitively for flowers and trees that had a special vital healing force. He then developed his famous Bach Flower Remedies. His work in treating patients for physical, emotional, and spiritual ailments was instrumental in bringing Dr. Aubrey T. Westlake into contact with these new methods of healing. Dr. Westlake studied fundamental theories about health and disease, starting with the writings of Hippocrates and ending with the research of Dr. Wilhelm Reich and his Orgone Theory. His search led him to healers using laying-on-of-hands, to the *kahunas* in Hawaii, and to J.E.R. McDonagh's Unitary Theory of Health and Disease. This resulted in Westlake's own book, *The Pattern of Health.* He then formed the Psionic Medical Society and Institute of Psionic Medicine, which brought together medical and homeopathic practicioners that utilized radiesthesia to its fullest extent. This group of professional men later wrote and published the book, *Psionic Medicine.*

The pendulum has come a long way since the first dowser used a forked stick or rock on a string to locate water. Even the name has changed: from dowsing to radiesthesia to psionic healing. But the science and art remains basically the same, whether in the hands of a professional or a layman. The pendulum is a remarkable tool capable of uncovering hitherto unknown facts. It can bring relief from illness as well as maintain good health. Anyone wishing to learn the pendulum's immense potential and develop his own capacity in its use must approach the subject with seriousness and respect. In turn it will reward him with many new insights into existing conditions. It can be used as a key to unlock the door of truth into many otherwise inaccessible areas of our everyday lives.

Updated New Dimensions

I have worked with the pendulum for a number of years, and during this time certain questions and limitations were discovered. I felt a need for these to be investigated through further research. I therefore have done some intensive psychic investigation and arrived at new insights and techniques. These are shared here, as I feel they have considerable value and add new dimensions and potential to the science and art of the pendulum.

* * * * *

Why Sometimes the Pendulum Does Not Work

Let me take a moment to explain that there are certain circumstances when you can not get readings or obtain accurate results. Sometimes the pendulum will not respond to questions, will act as if it is sluggish, will barely move, or will simply hang still. Audible music, for instance, seems to confuse the readings. You will find it much easier to work when you turn off the music. The pendulum won't work if there is an electrical storm, an earthquake, tidal waves, volcanic eruptions, or atomic testing in your area, as these events will disturb the electromagnetic energy field of the earth. There will be a time period during and after any such disruption in which you can not get accurate readings.

Also, if you are extremely tired or very ill and have a high fever you should not try to use the pendulum. You are working through the nervous system in your body, and when you are exhausted or out of balance you may not get accurate readings. You would be forcing yourself to really concentrate, so work when you are fresh and alert. However, when you feel an illness coming on it is still possible to use the pendulum and get a few quick answers to help yourself. However, any prolonged work would not be advisable.

Another time when you will find it difficult to take readings on yourself or another is after a laying-on-of-hands treatment. This can put so much energy into the body that it is not possible to get a steady reading. This is due to the fact that the healing energy is still working and conditions are changing. This can last as long as three days in the case of psychic surgery. The pendulum will actually show this by changing its way of swinging, indicating the changing conditions in the body.

* * * * *

**How Not To Use
the Pendulum**

Before discussing some of the infinite uses of the pendulum, I should mention another area that one should avoid because it does not deal with facts; that is predicting the future. If you misuse the pendulum in this way you are going to be on the Ouiji-board level: you will be engaged in trying to find out when you are going to die, whether you should marry someone, and other types of fortune-telling. If you merely play with the pendulum, as if it were a game, the results will be superficial and you will only get what is in your own subsconscious. When used properly, the pendulum tunes into the universal consciousness where the energy of intelligence will bring forth the right information.

Those who work at predicting the future know that the time element is the most difficult to forecast. The only time the pendulum can tell you something in the immediate future is when the information is already present in the human consciousness, as for instance during an election. You can not get an accurate reading before people have made up their minds, but when the votes are in but have not yet been counted or announced, the answer is there and the pendulist can pick it up accurately. You can test this also at a trial when the jury is working towards a decision; but again, you will not get an accurate reading before the members of the jury have made up their minds. Then you are picking up what is already known, but you are not really predicting. Thus if you want to know your own subconscious it is easy, but then you are dealing only with the content of your own consciousness, and not with objective knowledge. When the pendulist works objectively, new facts can be discovered that were previously completely unknown to him.

[1]Tomlinson, Dr. H. *Aluminum Utensils and Disease.* C.W. Daniel Co. Ltd., 1958. The dangers inherent in the widespread use of the metal.
[2]—. *The Divination of Disease.* Health Science Press, 1935. A study in Radiesthesia.

CHAPTER TWO

The Science of the Pendulum

The Pendulum

A pendulum can be almost any object suspended from a flexible link. However, for precise work with substances and colors, your pendulum should be of a neutral, non-conductive (of electricity) material such as wood, glass, or plastic, and it should be colorless, clear, or black. It can be made of an alloy of metals, since this is not found in nature and will be neutral. It should not be of a specific metal or have color, because then it would act as a sample which the operator would detect instead of being the medium between the pendulist and the sample. Some pendulums have a screw top and are hollow so that a sample can be placed inside that is similar to a material for which one is searching. The pendulum should be light, not too heavy or cumbersome, round or pear-shaped, and pointed at the bottom. See Diagram 1 on the next page. A pendulum made by the author is included with this course.

Diagram 1

8

PENDULUMS

Author's Pendulum
Actual Size

Screwtop Sample Pendulum

Dowsing Pendulum

Learning How To Use the Pendulum

Almost anyone can learn to use a pendulum to some extent, provided they practice, apply self-discipline, and remain aware of what they are doing. It will, of course, take some people longer to learn than others, because they may need more guidance and practice. As in anything else, some people will become more adept, since talent is always an important factor. Most people, however, can learn to use the pendulum for quick, simple, precise, factual answers, even if they do not wish to make a lifetime study of all the possibilities and uses described in this book.

Every object, animate or inanimate, gives off radiations, and our senses can feel and measure these to some extent. Our bodies receive these radiations just as a radio or television set receives its signals, and we can become like a telephone, so to speak, the recipient of information not available in any other way. The positive and negative poles of a magnet have their counterparts in the human body: the left side of the body is negative and the right side positive, with a neutral space in the center. And that is exactly how your mind has to be: neutral, quiet, in a questioning state, never letting thought or desire interfere with or influence the answer you seek! This is the most important thing to remember when you use a pendulum: have your mind in an "I don't know" attitude! If a condition was negative yesterday, I really don't know about it today; it may be the same, it may have improved or regressed. Whenever you work, only you will know whether you are doing this. You must be aware of your emotions and of what your mind is doing at the time you question. Any thoughts about a possible answer, any personal desires, and any ego involvement or tendency to show-off will influence your work. But if you question in complete objectivity the answer can and must be trusted. If you are not sure of the result after taking a reading, or your mind says "I thought this would be the answer," you may have influenced it. Go back and do it again; test it in another way, verify your answer. You can learn to be objective. After you have worked with the pendulum a while you will gain confidence. Start with some of the simple exercises given here and then move on to more complex work. When you finally proceed to areas where you may be emotionally involved, you will find that you can work on them objectively as well.

Enthusiasm and Confidence

Approach the pendulum with enthusiasm and with the confidence that you are able to do it. A half-hearted or doubtful attitude will only result in uncertain findings. Always work in quiet surroundings by yourself if at all possible, away from sceptics, negative thoughts, or anyone trying to influence you.

The Spectrum of Consciousness

I will be speaking of positive and negative conditions that relate to work with the pendulum, so I will clarify these. Though there are positive and negative poles in a magnet and the body itself has its own magnetic field, I will be using the terms positive and negative to identify certain segments of the spectrum of consciousness. As I see it, consciousness extends over a vast spectrum. Each of us as an individual has a personal frequency in which we live. We can function within a certain frequency range in the overall spectrum of consciousness. To remain in a state of health one must stay within one's optimum range. Certain conditions around us (which include food, clothing, and shelter) can change our frequency to such an extent that a condition of dis-ease occurs. In others words, things in our environment sometimes lower our frequency below our level of tolerance, thereby creating an unhealthful state. It is wise to check out the environment in which we spend most of our time, as well as the various types of food which make up the bulk of our diet. Once it has been established, we can stay within our healthy frequency range without having to constantly check everything out.

*　　*　　*　　*　　*

The Language of the Pendulum

The language of the pendulum may differ depending upon the person from whom you have learned the technique. Different systems interpret the various swings differently, or use the identification counting method. However you interpret, the system will work for you as long as its meaning is clear to you and your interpretation is constant. The method most generally used at present in the United States and Canada is the one described in this book.

There are four different swings. Whenever you hold the pendulum over any object, animate or inanimate, it will pick up radiations from it and begin to oscillate, first away from you and then back towards you. This is the neutral swing, which merely puts you in contact with the object. As soon as you ask a question the pendulum will answer by rotating. If it rotates to the right, clockwise, it is saying 'yes'; this is the positive swing, indicating a positive condition. If it rotates to the left, counterclockwise, it is saying 'no'; this is the negative swing, indicating a negative condition. If you ask a question which does not have a yes or no answer, which is confused, or in fact has no answer at all—for instance when asking about an appendix that has been removed—the pendulum will oscillate back and forth horizontally from right to left, meaning 'no answer'. You may have made a simple mistake, so try rephrasing your question more clearly.

The degree to which the pendulum rotates will indicate the extent of your answer. It may show you a small negative circular motion, as if it is saying, "Don't worry too much about this condition," while a large circular motion might mean, "Watch out, trouble." It might show a small, "Yes" swing or a very large, "Hallelujah, everything couldn't be better" 100% swing. The larger the swing the faster the pendulum seems to rotate, as if emphasizing the answer.

*   *   *   *   *

Various Uses of the Pendulum

There are basically four different ways in which to use the pendulum:

1. The pendulum is held directly over an object or body and questions asked concerning this object or body.
2. The pendulum is held over an object (like food or a remedy) which is held in your left hand and questions asked regarding the object's relationship to yourself.
3. A screwtop sample pendulum is used to dowse for a like substance.
4. The "Witness Method" is used which makes it possible to work for yourself or for someone else who may be present or at a distance. Witnesses (described later) are used for questioning and working in greater detail by using lists of words.

Each of these uses is discussed in detail in the following sections.

*   *   *   *   *

The First Way To Use the Pendulum

The direct method is the simplest way to start using the pendulum and to get used to it, gaining confidence as you work. Start by holding it over objects around your house and checking to see whether they give off positive or negative vibrations. Try any rocks, artifacts, or ancient relics to see if they show any negativity. You may decide not to wear old jewelry anymore or perhaps not to keep some old pot, painting, or treasure around any longer. Anything which gives off positive vibrations is good to keep close to you in your surroundings.

Try checking the difference in the degree of the swing when you hold it over a plant or flowers, some of which may be doing better than others. A just-opened flower will give a stronger reading than one which is beginning to wither.

It is very important to check your household products, your cosmetics and soaps, your cleansers, and anything with deodorants in it. So many of the products we use today contain harmful chemicals and could be the causes of allergies, rashes, or even low energy.

Animal Tests

You can test animals as well, using the pendulum over your pets. On one egg ranch in Southern California the pendulum is used over eggs to see whether the egg is fertile or not, and also whether it contains a male or a female chick; in this way the egg production at the ranch has been increased tremendously. (Incidentally, they found out that the women working there could go up to six hours, with regular breaks, before losing accuracy in their work.)

Sex Determination

In a similar way, the sex of an unborn child or animal can easily be determined by using the positive swing for male, the negative swing for female. In the case of multiple birth, it is also possible to find out by careful questioning how many males and females are in an animal's litter; first establish how many there are in all by asking if there are 1, 2, 3, etc., then how many males and how many females.

The Fertility Cycle

Some women use the pendulum to establish times of highest and lowest fertility for either conception or birth control. This is all right as long as you are not influencing the answer by your desire for the enjoyment of sex! Ask, "Is this a good or a bad day?" A calendar can be used to find out individual cycles.

Direction-finding

When you are outdoors, your pendulum can be used to tell you where north is. Simply ask this, point your arm, and turn slowly around in a circle. The pendulum will then oscillate until you notice a large swing indicating north and a shorter one pointing to the south. You can then check the exact direction by asking for the largest positive swing. This can be very helpful when you are out camping or in a strange environment, but test it before you get lost! The pendulum indicates direction because you are working with the electromagnetic energy of the earth, which runs from north to south.

Harmful Radiations

You will find it very interesting to test your television set to see how far it gives off harmful radiations. Turn it on and start right at the screen to pick up your negative swing, then see how far out it goes before the pendulum shows neutral again. It may extend as far as several feet, depending on the size of the set and the strength of the tubes. Also check at each side to see how wide the negative angle is. Don't sit within that negative zone close to the set, or let your children or animals sit within this area because they are going to pick up the harmful radiations.

It also happens that some places or houses, or even whole streets, give off harmful radiations due to a certain kind of subterranean water or a negative magnetic field. This situation may result in the inhabitants picking up harmful emanations which cause illness and lack of sleep. A competent pendulist will have to find a way to get rid of the cause, if possible.

*   *   *   *   *

Direct Diagnosis From the Human Body

By holding the pendulum over the body, you can detect any energy distortion indicating an imbalance. Begin by picking up the neutral swing. The energy normally flows up and down the body and follows any curve, such as a bent arm. You can detect negative conditions in the body involving an organ or a gland by inquiring about functions and systems while moving the pendulum slowly over the part and asking appropriate questions. Remember, however, that a pain may give a negative energy distortion reading in one area, but this may be a reflex only, with the cause being in another part of the body. A headache, for instance, may be caused by a digestive problem.

You can check this method on yourself by making the following little test. If there is nothing wrong with your arm, give it a good slap; you will immediately be able to take a negative distortion reading which shows that there is an energy loss at this point. You can see exactly how far this reaches up and down the arm, showing the extent of the little injury. As it is a very minor one, the pendulum will slow down in its rotation almost immediately and within a minute or so return to its normal neutral swing, indicating that the trouble is resolved.

*   *   *   *   *

How To Make a Cursory Evaluation of Body Conditions

By holding the pendulum over the tips and other points of the fingers of either hand as shown in the following diagram, you can determine the state of health or disease in the body. This is very helpful in finding out quickly about the major systems, functions, and conditions of the physical body. (It is not always possible to have your equipment available, such as in an emergency when you need some quick answers.) This method uses the points in the hand which reflect from the various parts of the body, and you are, of course, not measuring the hand itself. This will tell you about the acid-alkaline balance in the body and also about the condition of the heart and the blood circulation. Furthermore, you can determine the level of physical energy in the body, as well as the etheric energy, which always gives a higher reading since it feeds the physical body. Only in cases of shock or out-of-the-body states will the etheric energy get dangerously low, below the level of the physical energy. Just before death, the etheric energy will disappear completely—in fact, before the physical body takes its last breath.

I have done very careful psychic investigation into finding these reflex points in the hand, and researched them extremely thoroughly. It is a very convenient method when you can not hold the pendulum directly over the body. See Diagram 2 on the next page for a summary of this, and begin to memorize the energy distortion points in the hand.

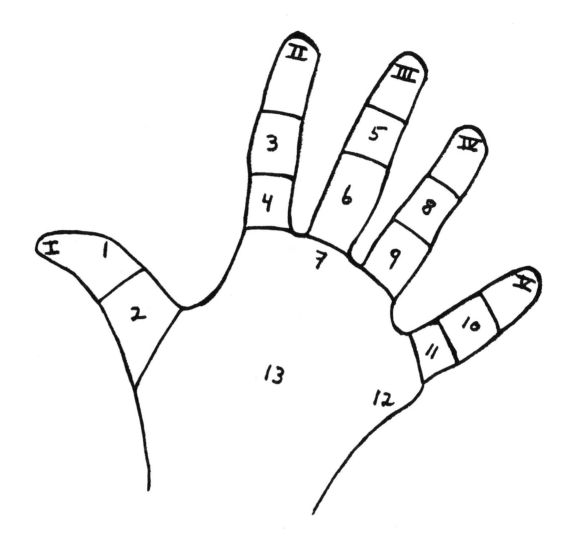

I	NERVOUS SYSTEM — Brain — Physical Energy
	1 Etheric Energy
	2 Acid Alkali Balance
II	RESPIRATORY SYSTEM
	3 Bronchial
	4 Lungs
III	DIGESTIVE SYSTEM
	5 Liver
	6 Stomach
	7 Intestines
IV	URINARY SYSTEM
	8 Kidneys
	9 Bladder
V	REPRODUCTIVE SYSTEM
	10 Male: Testes — Prostate
	Female: Uterus — Ovaries
	11 Genitals
12	BLOOD CONDITION & CIRCULATION
13	HEART FUNCTION

**Schematic
Testing**

If you are having trouble with the electrical system of your automobile, your television set, or radio, you can find a short-circuit or some other problem by holding the pendulum directly over a diagram or schematic of that piece of equipment.

In Europe, the pendulum is used more in laboratories than it is in the United States, although this kind of use is beginning here also.

It is possible to find lost objects or people with the pendulum by using a diagram or map; the police can be aided in this way, too. However, if a "Witness" of the lost person is used it is usually more successful.

It is a simple matter to detect whether or not a document is a forgery. For instance, a positive swing indicates a genuine letter, signature, or will.

The pendulum has also been used (mostly in Europe) to find out certain characteristics about a person by utilizing a sample of a person's handwriting as a "Witness."

**Testing Your
Accuracy**

An interesting test of one's accuracy can easily be performed by checking separate papers with mathematical calculations, some correct and some with errors. Mix them up, place them face down on a table, and find the correct ones through positive readings and the incorrect ones by negative readings. This, of course, can be most helpful if you are doing actual mathematical work.

The same type of test can similarly be applied to oneself, in any variation of the old 'shell game'. However, that is getting into those types of very boring ESP tests that parapsychologists love to invent. Personally, I have found that the psychic faculties work best and enable the person to obtain the most accurate readings when one has a good reason or there is a strong tie-in with the object of one's search. Many psychics have found that under strict laboratory conditions they can not "perform," as it seems to have a curtailing effect on their intuitive factor; there is also pressure felt due to the fact that one is supposed to prove something at all costs. Therefore, if you find it difficult to prove your accuracy under test conditions, do not let it discourage you.

*   *   *   *   *

The Second Way To Use the Pendulum

In order to find out about food or any other products such as vitamins, herbs, remedies, etc. in relationship to yourself, hold the object in your left hand and test by holding the pendulum over it. In this way—even if a particular object or food is giving a positive reading—you can find out your own particular relationship to it by holding it yourself. Your answer, however, is for the immediate time only; it might be different at another time, with regard to this particular food. This will be explored a little later. This second method is only used for a quick and simple yes or no answer, which can then be worked out in further detail by using the "Witness" method.

This second method can also be applied in working for another person; have them hold an object, food, or remedy in their hand while you are holding the pendulum over it and ask the necessary questions. If that person is asleep or too ill, or somehow incapable of holding the object himself, you can still question for him. This is done by holding the remedy in your own hand, keeping the pendulum between their body and the remedy, while taking your readings for them.

In both these cases, while taking readings for yourself or for another, you simply ask the question: "Is this good for me, for him or her?" If the answer is no, you naturally look for something else that can be helpful. If you get a yes, you can find out the exact quantity that is needed. The pendulum will give you a yes answer as you build up the quantity by asking 1, 2, 3, etc., then give you a neutral swing when you have overstepped the amount, indicating that the remedy will no longer do any good. It will even go to a negative swing if you continue, thereby acting as a safeguard and indicating that this will have to be thrown off by the body, as it is a harmful amount. After finding out the right amount, you can then check further how often it should be taken; although it is difficult to check too far ahead, and better to recheck this again to see if conditions have changed to give another answer. This system may work even better when you use the "Witness" method because there are many more details you can work out. It is not always convenient for the patient or yourself to stand there asking a lot of questions.

* * * * *

The Third Way To Use the Pendulum

The terms sample and witness must not be confused, as is sometimes the case. They are not the same, nor are they used in the same manner. A sample is a fragment or part of the material for which one is searching. It is used inside a hollow screwtop pendulum which can be held over a map or over the ground when prospecting. It can contain liquids such as water or oil, or a fragment of a certain material one is specifically looking for. In this way the sample pendulum with the enclosed material is aligned with the substance of the quest. This is a separate use for the sample pendulum only, in which that particular pendulum is used as a "Witness" and not as an intermediate tool between the pendulist and the person for whom you work.

*   *   *   *   *

The Fourth Way To Use the Pendulum

I will now explain the equipment, or materials, used in the "Witness" method, which is the most complex. The materials required include a "Determination Board" and "Pointer," a magnet, and "Witnesses;" it also includes lists of "Work Pages" and "Anatomy Charts." These are all included with this course. The use of each of these will be described in detail. You will then have at your disposal a most interesting and rewarding method, one in which the pendulum can be your informer and you can utilize it to its fullest potential.[1]

*   *   *   *   *

[1]To order any additional books, pendulums, materials, or copies of the work-list pages and anatomy charts see the enclosed order form, or write to IDYLWILD BOOKS.

The Witnesses

There are two kinds of witnesses, primary and secondary. A primary witness is something that ties the pendulist in with the person for whom he is working, be it yourself or someone else. It can be any object which has been handled by the person, such as a photograph (a negative is even better), a signature, preferably in pencil (ink has a strong vibration of its own), a bit of clothing, some hair, etc. Sputum on a piece of absorbent paper is also good but lasts only a short time. The very best primary witness is a spot of blood, since it keeps its vital radiation for many years and is as personal as a fingerprint. However, the pendulist is not analyzing the blood of a person when using a blood-spot as a primary witness, it merely ties him in to all that is going on in the sphere of that person. I personally prefer to use a blood-spot, and it is also absolutely essential for use in "Broadcasting," which will be gone into later. Do not use bodily waste products; those are used in black magic, which is never concerned with healing. Stay in the white, or "Light magic," which is for the benefit of the patient.

To make a blood-spot-witness, prick a finger and put a drop of blood on a small absorbent paper such as rice paper, tissue, or paper towel. This should be placed immediately in a small cellophane envelope (available in stamp shops) and taped shut with scotch tape. If you do not have any cellophane at hand, you could fold the blood-spot in a small square of wax paper or plastic, but do not put it in any material that is too thick. You can also have the person initial it, since all blood-spots tend to look alike. A more lasting way is to keep it in a file with the person's name, together with other charts you might make for him. A paper clip will easily keep it inside an ordinary manila file.

A secondary witness is used to work on a specific problem for the primary witness (yourself or another person). Secondary witnesses are the names of things: diseases, conditions, harmful materials in the body, or the names of a part of the body, or of a system or function that needs specific attention. Furthermore, secondary witnesses are also the names of colors, remedies, or procedures which are indicated by the pendulum, and which are used to counteract a specific negative condition and help to change that negative condition to a positive one.

Such secondary witnesses can be made simply by writing the necessary word in pencil on a slip of paper. They are usually written up specifically as needed in your investigation. It is helpful to always keep slips of paper at hand for this purpose. A Witness

Folder is included with this course containing envelopes for the blood-spot-witnesses, and 50 of the most used witnesses.

*   *   *   *   *

The Determination Board

The Determination Board is of a neutral material and is designed to work out details for a primary witness. The board should be used on a wooden desk or table; and the pendulist should face north, if possible, in order to align himself with the north-south magnetic flow of the earth. There should be no metal objects underneath or near the board to disturb the vibrations of the witnesses being used. The person you work for need not be present, as the primary witness ties him in to you, thereby making teleradiesthesia (or working at a distance) possible.

The determination board has two circles on it. The smaller one on top is the witness circle, in which the witnesses are placed. The lower circle on the determination board is marked in degrees from 0° to 360° in order to take numerical readings for purposes of accuracy and comparison. This circle is divided into 3 segments. A little further on in this book you will be able to see a correlation to a universal theme of 3 parts making up the whole.

The first segment of the circle ranges from 0° to 120°; any readings found in this segment are classified as indicating negative conditions. The two segments from 120° to 360°, comprising the remainder of the circle, are designated as giving positive readings.

Readings in the second segment, from 120° to 240°, indicate changeable conditions ranging from barely functional to only slightly imbalanced; i.e., the body is either just holding its own, is slipping into an unhealthful condition, or is in a stage of recovery.

The readings found within the third segment, from 240° to 360°, indicate a stable condition.

Remember, in using the determination board, the lower the reading, the worse or more aggravated the condition; while the higher

20

the reading, the more trouble-free and healthful the condition.

The purpose of using the determination board is to take numerical readings and find out precisely if a negative condition exists and to what extent it is affecting the body. The same method can then be used to find remedies that will raise the witness's frequency out of the state of imbalance and into a condition indicating more perfect health.

See Diagram 3 on the next page of the determination board which shows the witness circle and the three segments of the circle of degrees.

A determination board and pointer is included with this course.

Diagram 3

THE DETERMINATION BOARD

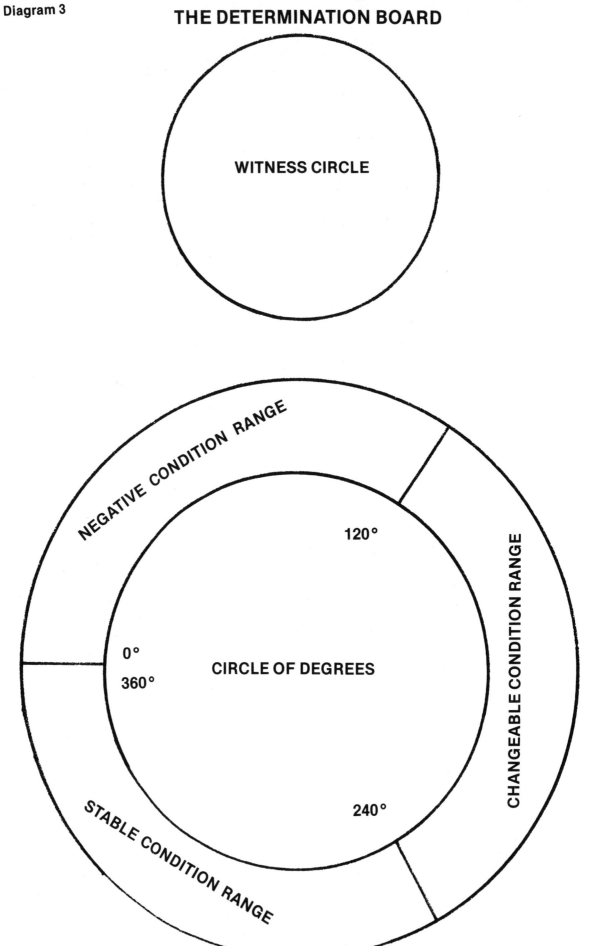

WITNESS CIRCLE

NEGATIVE CONDITION RANGE

CHANGEABLE CONDITION RANGE

120°

0°

360°

CIRCLE OF DEGREES

240°

STABLE CONDITION RANGE

The Use of Lists

In order to avoid having to think up innumerable names or questions which keep one's mind occupied, it is extremely helpful to use written words and lists. These can be words written in pencil, typed, or printed. But you should not use a page in a book, since you would pick up words from the other side of the page with their own vibrations. The list or words must be placed on a black surface or paper that blocks out other vibrations in order to get a clear reading from the single word you need. These Work-List Pages which are included in this course (and a black paper) have been revised and are now on 8½ x 11 paper. The simplest way to use the Work-List Pages is to use plastic page-protectors which come with a black separation paper in them. You can place two consecutively numbered pages in one of them. They are 3-holed, as the Work-List Pages are, and can easily be put into a binder for convenience, thus keeping all of the course papers together.

Each of the Work-List Pages will be discussed and clarified.

*   *   *   *   *

The Pointer

A stick of neutral material such as wood or plastic is used for pointing to words. Hold it in your left hand and point to one word at a time, asking for a correlation; i.e., while pointing to the word and focusing your mind on the question, ask whether that condition exists in regard to the primary witness in a negative or a positive way. Any negative correlation has to be looked at and worked on further, and a remedy sought for it. When a negative condition is found, and by using its name as a secondary witness (as will be described later), one can then look for a positive reading by pointing to a possible remedy or procedure. Finally, by making the chosen remedy into a witness, you can place it with the other witnesses in the witness circle and determine exactly how it should be used for the specific condition; you can also determine how much of it should be used and how often. Whenever you add another witness to the primary witness you are trying to zero in on that specific condition or purpose and you are filling in details about it to a very fine degree.

You can make a pointer out of any stick or wood. One simple

way is to prepare a wooden chopstick by sharpening the end in a pencil sharpener. Chopsticks are available in healthfood stores and oriental shops. A pointer is included with this course.

*   *   *   *   *

The Use of a Clearing Magnet

With the foregoing tools you can now begin to take quantitative readings on a condition, either negative or positive. There is, however, one more essential step to take; before placing a primary witness in the witness circle of the determination board, you must clear the board of any vibrations which might have remained from a previous primary witness, or from you handling the board. In order to clear the witness circle, take a magnet and rub it in a circular, counter clockwise motion a couple of times inside the witness circle. Then place the primary witness in the witness circle and rub across it once with the magnet to remove your own vibrations.

A 1 oz. horseshoe magnet is included with this course.

*   *   *   *   *

How To Take Numerical Readings

First, hold your pendulum over the witness and pick up the radiation in its neutral swing. As soon as you ask a question or point to a word related to the information you are requesting, the pendulum will change to either a positive or a negative swing, thus indicating 'yes' or 'no' with regard to that specific question. Remember, your body is like a magnet; since the left hand can receive impressions, you can therefore also use it to point to the words questions. The right hand is on the positive side of the body, except when the person is left-handed (in which case the body's polarity may be reversed). From the need of the primary witness and through the questioning process, the pendulum will act as an indicator of the information sought. Also remember that your mind must be as quiet and neutral as the center of a magnet, resembling a telephone which merely transmits information without coloring or changing it in any way. Since you want your mind to be as quiet and neutral as possible, it is much better to use lists of names so that your mind is not working needlessly all the time. When completely relaxed, the mind can be used intuitively and intelligently to ask the right questions as you search for ways to change negative conditions into positive, healthful ones.

After receiving the first indicated reading, whether positive or negative (and if you do not want a quantitative answer), you can go on to the next word. For instance, if you get a positive swing on a disease, it means that the primary witness (the person you are working on) is not afflicted with that problem and you need go no further—unless it is a special condition that you have been attempting to improve. If you want to obtain a quantitative reading, or compare this reading to an earlier one, you use the following procedure.

The Demarcation Procedure

Move the pendulum down and across the 120° line of demarcation (between the positive and negative reading segments), to the 0° point; it will continue its initial swing, whether negative or positive, as you pause there for a moment. Then move the pendulum slowly and rhythmically around the circle clockwise, without any jerking, until it begins to oscillate in the neutral swing: indicating the degree reading. As soon as it has stopped rotating and changed to an oscillating movement (the neutral swing) it is a simple matter to align it with the degree line marked on the circle. Each degree line is at a slightly different angle and shows a specific numerical reading. At this point, if you have gone a little too fast or too slow, it is all right to move the pendulum forward or backward in order to line it up with the reading, because the pendulum has already set its direction and will continue to oscillate (marking the degree line in the air above the board, as it were). It will not waver from this degree line until you discontinue and go back to the witness circle for the next reading. This whole procedure is done just above the witness and the board and has to be repeated every time. It is necessary to go through this demarcation procedure each time to take an accurate reading. See Diagram 4 on the next page showing how to use the pendulum over the determination board.

Diagram 4

HOW TO TAKE READINGS

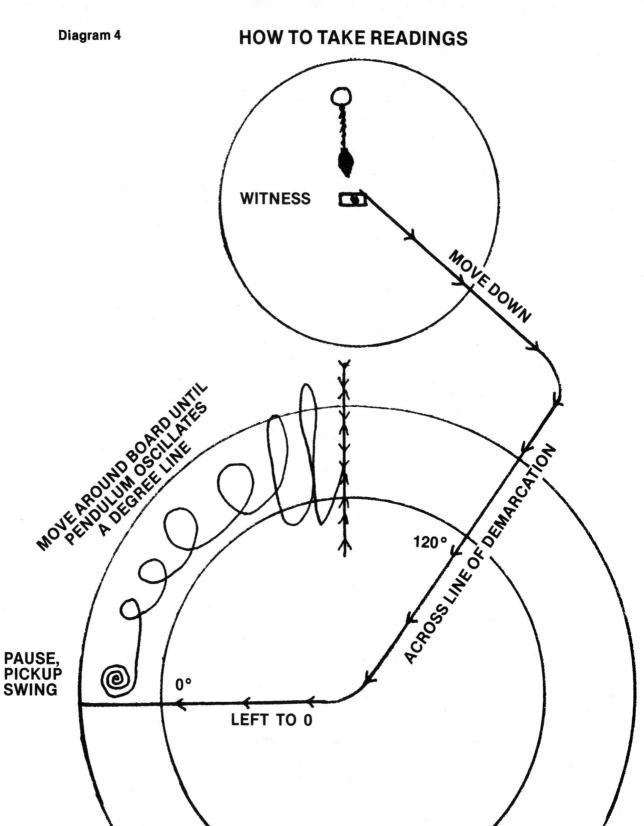

WITNESS

MOVE DOWN

MOVE AROUND BOARD UNTIL PENDULUM OSCILLATES A DEGREE LINE

ACROSS LINE OF DEMARCATION

120°

0°

PAUSE, PICKUP SWING

LEFT TO 0

**Negative
Readings**

You will find that negative readings range from 0° to 120° in this procedure. The only exception occurs in extremely serious cases; here the pendulum will go all the way around the circle of degrees in the negative swing (moving in very large fast circles) sometimes several times, and then stop in the same negative segment. Add 360° (for each time it has gone around) to the number of the degree where it finally stops for the correct reading.

**Positive
Readings**

All positive readings will lie in the range from 120° to 360°. By using the determination board you can check on the way in which a condition has changed compared to the last time you worked on it to see if it has remained the same, or if it is regressing or improving. In this way, the pendulum can tell you many things in great detail and provide a total picture of the situation and condition of any particular person. By this method, you will also learn if what you are attempting to do for yourself or another is valuable, or if you must seek further help from other sources.

*   *   *   *   *

**An Interesting
Exception**

Occasionally, it will seem that the pendulum's initial swing is wavering between positive to negative, as if unable to decide. This could mean that you can not obtain a reading at that particular time due to changing conditions (as discussed earlier). It could also indicate that the condition is just around 120° and is either just improving and ready to move from negative to positive, or is just beginning to get out of balance, as for instance when an illness is coming on. In such a case, if you have been working on something, pick up the negative swing and see how close to 120° it registers—perhaps it is 115° and about to become positive. When you encounter this undecided swing with regard to something upon which you have not previously been working, it is an indication that something is beginning to fall into a negative state. It may be a prediction that a mild illness is beginning. You can also pick up the positive swing and see how close to 120° the pendulum will register. It may want to stop in the negative segment (again probably around 115°), indicating that there is something to be concerned about. This should be corrected as soon as possible in order to prevent the development of a more severe problem, which of course is harder to correct.

* * * * *

Conditions in the Etheric Body

The pendulum reveals not only actual physical conditions, it will also disclose conditions in the etheric body through which the distribution of vital energy is channeled to our glandular system. Some readings may pertain to conditions existing only on the etheric level and as yet not present in the gross physical body. Other readings may reveal conditions which are latent or about to come down into the physical. Such readings show imbalances in the etheric which will bring on disease (or "miasms" as they are called in homeopathy), i.e., hereditary conditions and predispositions indicating inherent weaknesses that may show up at times of stress, imbalance, or a virus attack. The pendulist must check to see whether the conditions found to be negative are actually in the physical body or are latent tendencies. If there are no symptoms or any discomfort the conditions may still be only in the etheric body. If this is the case, it acts as a warning signal, and counter measures can be taken to prevent that particular weakness from materializing in the physical body. This is easily verified by asking or pointing to the words 'physical' or 'predisposition', the 'physical body' or the 'etheric body', and reading the yes or no answer. See Work-List Page 1.

* * * * *

A Word of Caution and Advice

Since this book is written for everyone to read—the trained practitioner in orthodox methods of medicine as well as the layman—let me insert a word of caution for the non-professionals at this point. The law in the United States says that no one is allowed to diagnose or prescribe medicine unless one has a license to do so. Neither is anyone allowed to remove tissue from the body of a person or lay-on-hands unless one is a minister or has a specific license to do so (or does not charge for the laying-on-of-hands). This is, in itself, a very good precautionary law, since one should not become an overnight "pendulum quack!" The same is true in any study of the healing arts, whether it be therapy, homeopathy, herbs, massage, etc. If you have such a license and the knowledge that goes with it, what a great opportunity you have in learning the use of the pendulum to augment your methods! You can work your healing method from the preventive point of view and aid your patients in innumerable ways. This is what the Psionic medical group in England is doing, and there is no reason why it could not become a part of our healing practices in this country as well. Some individual doctors and healers in various professional capacities are using the pendulum already, sometimes without telling their patients, since they feel it might be frowned upon.

Non Interference With Physicians

If you are not a professional, never interfere with anything a doctor tells his patient. Do not have a patient discontinue any treatment or medication given by a doctor in favor of your recommended course of action. That would not only be highly irresponsible but possibly even dangerous in many cases. The decision is up to the patient; it is both his responsibility and his right to determine what he wishes to do with his body—whether it is to trust the healer of his choice or to receive other care. You should advise a patient to ask his doctor whether there is any reason why he should not discontinue a certain medication he is taking before making any decision.

If you are a layman, always be humble in your work, and be especially careful in what you tell another or what you offer to do for him. However, you can work with the pendulum to assist in the treatment being given by a physician. For example, if you or someone else is getting radiation treatments for cancer and you know that these deplete the body of certain vitamins, you can find out how much it will take to replenish that loss and maintain balance. Thus you would be working to maintain health, and you would be counteracting side-effects and reinstating deficiencies in the body by natural remedies which could never be considered in the same category as drugs.

Spiritual Healing and the Natural Ways

We all have a right to do with our bodies what we want or think is best for us. We can take professional treatments and supplement them with good, basic health practices. We have the right to believe that natural methods and remedies such as vitamins, nutrients, herbs, biochemic cell salts, packs, baths, exercise, massage, yoga, etc., are beneficial, and we can choose to explore and use them. Many people, including doctors, are turning away today from the practice of prescribing and experimenting only with drugs, since they are not successful in many instances in treating the cause of the illness. At present, one can go into any drugstore and buy thousands of really harmful, strong chemicals (called medicines) without prescription. These throw our bodies completely out of balance, can change our own natural functions and rhythms, and cut down our natural defences. They are the cause of more harm than good, even if they do alleviate symptoms temporarily or lesson our pain. But one has a choice regarding all of this; many people are choosing spiritual healing and the natural ways for themselves and for their families.

**A Moral
Law**

Do not work for others unless they have asked you to do so, for you would be interfering in their lives. If, however, that person is already in your care it would be all right, as in the case of a small child for whom you are responsible, or a close friend with whom you have rapport. If you work for others without their permission you are going to get into all kinds of difficulties, and not just legally. They may not believe you, they will not do anything for themselves or cooperate in any way, and you will have not only wasted your time but will have created further problems. It is a very good moral law to work only for those who ask you, as this will tie you in with them through mutual interest, respect, and love. That is the only beneficial climate in which healing can take place.

It is not your responsibility to heal anyone! It is the God force, the Divine Intelligence, their acceptance of the universal truth and the Light that heals—not you. You can heal no one; they heal themselves. Just as a simple cut will heal by itself, so is there healing available at the right time and at the right place, and at the right moment of love. No one really knows when or how or why it is so. All one can do is to work with the greatest humility as best one can, knowing that it is never up to the healer to heal, but up to the patient to receive healing in his own moment of truth. Someone will ask you to work for them if they are open to natural methods and are really looking for a way in which to take responsibility and help themselves. Then you may be able to point something out to them which will be helpful.

**Willingness
To Change**

However, there is nothing the healer can do to counteract what the patient will not do for himself! For instance, if he has emphysema and will not stop smoking, there is little you can do. Miracle healings do occur, but if the patient continues to do the very things that brought him to ill health or dis-ease, the illness will come back—and it usually comes back much more severely because he knows what he is doing that is causing the problem. Spend your time and energy on the patient who is honestly willing to change his way of life. Work with him, tell him perhaps about an article you read, or an incident from your own experience. Then you can test to see what is needed by the witness method of the pendulum, to see how this applies in his case at that time. There is nothing harmful in pointing out natural means of maintaining health or countering ill health; then you are leaving the decision to the patient, as to whether he wants to do anything or not.

**Part of a
Holistic Method**
The lay pendulist can find appropriate remedies as long as he asks the patient what he is already taking or doing, and then works to find what else would be absolutely safe in this particular instance. By using that information as a secondary witness, you can ask the pendulum to work out other things that would be safe and helpful. This is, or course, what any good practitioner would do—questioning the patient regarding his history and the medication he is taking.

Thus the pendulistic method could and should be a part of a holistic approach to health care. The efficacy of any single method of healing is limited, no matter how good it may be in itself. The current trend in our society is towards holistic healing, and the pendulist can help to provide holistic health-care and be a pioneer in research along these lines. These are the highest of moral and spiritual goals, and should be an inspiration to all who work in the science and art of pendulum healing. Working with the pendulum implies using it to its highest and fullest capacity to aid and maintain the natural balance of things. Health is natural; ill health is not. Balance is the order that nature strives for, and imbalance is a distortion of that order.

*   *   *   *   *

**Principles
Involved in
Health and
Disease**
The professional radiesthetists who use Psionic methods of healing today are treating the underlying causes of disease, not merely alleviating the symptoms. They can also recognize and find, through the use of the pendulum, hereditary predispositions (known as miasms in homeopathy). Furthermore, they realize that the residue of an illness, like a culture of bacteria,

can remain in the body as a toxin which causes illness. These concepts and principles are thoroughly discussed in *The Pattern of Health* and *Psionic Medicine*, which includes *Mc.Donagh's Unitary Concept of Disease.* The valuable book entitled *Some Unrecognized Factors in Medicine* has also aided me in the following explanations and diagrams. These books are fascinating studies for a pendulist, no matter what his previous background or training has been.

For a basic look at some of these principles, let us start by examining the activity of each protein molecule. See Diagram 5 on the next page concerning embryology.

Diagram 5   *33*

EMBRYOLOGY

Male Sperm   **Female Ova**

Embrio

Blastocyst

Estoderm   **Mesoderm**   **Endoderm**

Nervous System	Skeletal	Respiratory System
Sense Organs	Muscular	Digestive System
Epiderm	Circulatory	Alimentary Canal Linings
Brain	Excretory	Pharynx
Spinal Cord	Reproductive System	Thyroid
Hypophysis Cerebri	Muscular Tissues	Liver
Anus	Connective Tissues	Pancreas
etc.	Heart	Gall Bladder
	Blood Vessels & Organs	Larynx
	Lymph Vessels & Organs	Trachea
	Kidneys	Lungs
	Ureters	Urinary Bladder
	Testes	Female Urethra
	Ovaries	etc.
	Uterine Tubes	
	Serous Membranes	
	etc.	

PROTEIN MOLECULE

Epiblast   **Mesoblast**   **Hypoblast**

Attractor — Functioning   **Storer — Functioning**   **Radiator — Functioning**

Adrenal Gland	Ovaries	Parathyroid Gland
Medulla	Musco-Skeleton System	Blood
Skin	Testes	Thymus Gland
Eyes	Cardio-Vascular System	Respiratory System
Posterior Pituitary	Cortex of Suprarenal	Islets of Langerhans
Anterior Pituitary	Urogenital System	with Portal Systems
Nervous System		Thyroid Gland
Pineal Gland		

AMINO ACIDS

D N A	Protein Molecule	R N A
Genetic	**Biochemical**	**Dynamic**
Carrier of Information	**Substance To Genetic Pattern**	**Catalist Uniting D N A & Protein Molecule**
Wide Variety of Symptoms	**Deficiency Or Inferior Quality Of Cell Substance**	**Toxins**

A Universal Theme

Please note a fascinating, continuing theme: a trinity of three parts making up a whole, a theme which exists on all levels of the universe and in our total consciousness. You will see how this recurring theme runs through each explanation and each of the Diagrams. It shows the existence of a basic law of the universe—whether seen in function or perceived in order—and one that should encourage us to consider the human being a spiritual, emotional, and physical whole. Therefore, for healing to take place, there must be a harmony and balance between all three factors, and the approach used must always consider all three aspects. Holistic healing must encompass the three areas in which man functions: the physical, emotional, and mental. No single approach is completely effective, since all three parts must be considered and balanced.

An ancient theme in medicine (originating with Paracelsus and taken up by several medical philosophies right to the present day) is the concept that there is only one disease and one cure. To understand this basic concept of health, disease, and underlying causes as they relate to the protein molecule, see Diagram 6 on the next page, on health and disease.

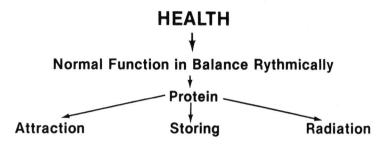

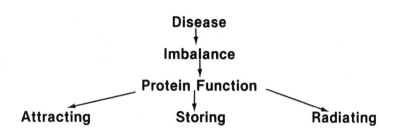

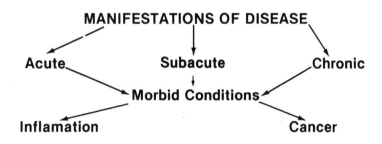

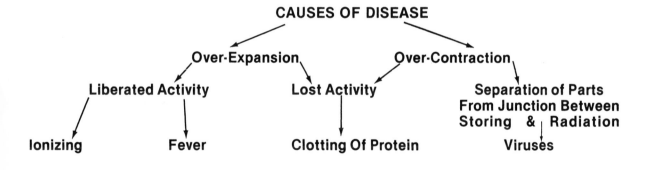

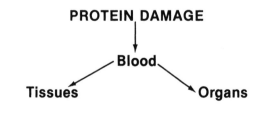

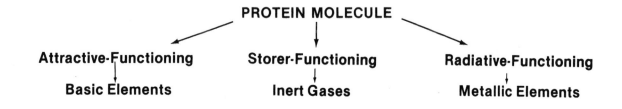

Miasms

The inherited predispositions known as miasms in homeopathy, and the miasms acquired from childhood illnesses, are the underlying causes of all future illness in the body. The theory of miasms explains why there seem to be tendencies which always lead to certain basic weaknesses and groups of diseases in the body. For instance, if one has the inherited miasm of tuberculosis, one will become ill in the respiratory system more readily than in other parts of the body, always being the first to catch cold, the first to get bronchitis, or the first to get lung infection. For further clarification about this and the three racial miasms in relation to nucleic cell energy and disordered activity in the body, see Diagram 7 on the next page.

Diagram 7 *37*

MIASMS

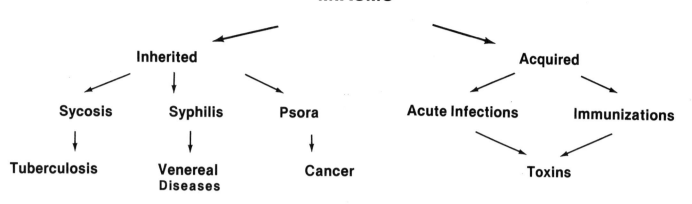

THREE RACIAL MIASMS

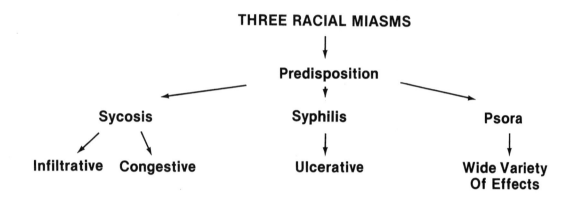

NUCLEIC CELL ENERGY

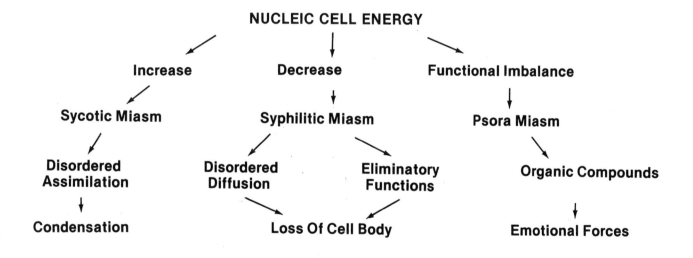

MIASMS CAUSE BLOCKAGES

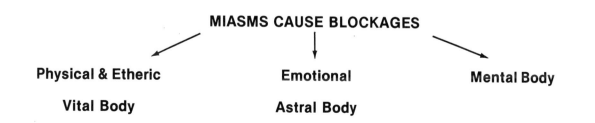

Karma　　　　　An ancient term for predisposition is karma. Karma can be thought of as the previous conditioning with which a person is born; this brings into play hereditary factors which influence the emotional nature. Recognizing this link can be helpful in understanding the total person. Karma is simply cause and effect over an extended period of time. Miasms are caused by physical illness, whereas karmic conditions are formed by emotional or psychological factors stemming from certain experiences. Today we are all quite familiar with the fact that emotional disturbances affect our physical well-being and can cause psychosomatic illness. If karma is thought of in these terms, it can be seen to tie-in also with the hereditary causes of imbalance, regardless of whether the hereditary factor is physically inherited from our parents or emotionally carried-over from past experience. Basically, there are three types of karma as shown in Diagram 8 on the next page.

Diagram 8

39

KARMA

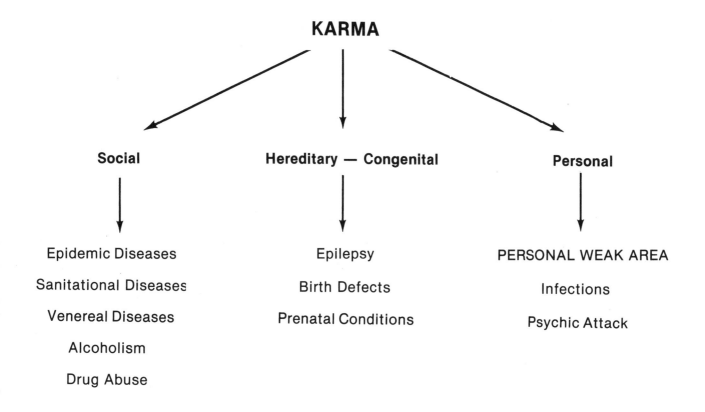

Social — **Hereditary — Congenital** — **Personal**

Epidemic Diseases / Epilepsy / PERSONAL WEAK AREA

Sanitational Diseases / Birth Defects / Infections

Venereal Diseases / Prenatal Conditions / Psychic Attack

Alcoholism

Drug Abuse

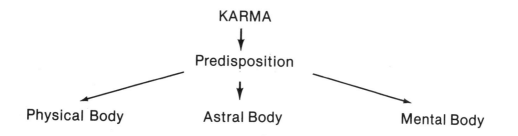

KARMA

Predisposition

Physical Body — Astral Body — Mental Body

BEHAVIOR DETERMINES

HEALTH — DISEASE

Please note the last category on the chart which truly states that no matter what the underlying cause of an imbalance is, your behavior, your actions, and the way you live determines the balance between health and disease. We are not slaves to any predisposition or condition. It is how we live, what we do, and how we act that will change our disorder into order. Therefore be very careful not to program your mind into accepting any existing condition as being inevitable or irreversible. Each moment is new and can be the beginning of a new life. If approached in that way, miracles in healing or regeneration can take place. The time to act is now, as any postponement further complicates any malfunction.

**Unified Concept
of Balance
and Imbalance**

By using the basic, unified concept of balance and imbalance, the pendulist can now begin to use the pendulum in an exciting new way: one involving a holistic approach to the total person which will create order and unity in him. This will invariably be reflected in all his relationships and lead to harmony and order in his surroundings. That is the real meaning and the real reason for being in good health: it benefits not only oneself but everyone with whom one has a relationship.

*   *   *   *   *

**The Use of
Anatomy Charts**

If you suspect some problem exists, are having discomfort or pain, or if you have found with the pendulum that there is something wrong in the body, you can use an anatomy chart to locate the trouble. There are eighteen anatomy charts included with this course. These can be put in plastic page-protectors like the Work-List Pages. By using the determination board and a primary witness, and then pointing to an appropriate anatomy chart, you can quickly locate any negative readings. By moving the pointer around the chart you can see where the negative reading originates and the extent to which surrounding areas are affected. Areas not affected will give a positive reading. The numerals on the charts will give you the name of an organ, a gland or part of the body if you are not familiar with it. You can then use that name as a secondary witness to find out what is wrong and what to do about it. The anatomy charts are also used for "Broadcasting" as described later.

For the basic knowledge of anatomy, an excellent book is *Atlas of Human Anatomy.''*

I will now begin the explanation of each of the 15 Work-List Pages, which are described in detail in the following two chapters. These Work-List Pages are included with this course.

CHAPTER THREE

Working With the Pendulum

Work-List Page 1

Work-List Page 1 is a basic questions and information work page. This is the starting point in your work; it contains key words and other useful information to which you will find references over and over again. This information will then lead to other pages for further detailed information lists to complete the inquiry as needed. Page 1 gives basic information which must be consulted as a first step to see if there are any negative conditions in a major system, in parts, or in glands of the body. Page 1 also lists some questions concerning the patient himself, such as whether you should or should not work for him; whether there will be cooperation; the extent of his pain; his blood count; whether there is over-activity or under-activity in his systems, glands, and functions, etc. Then the names of the affected parts can be used as secondary witnesses as you work on other Work-List pages for further information and in greater detail.

*   *   *   *   *

Work-List Pages 2 and 3

To find out the name of an illness, "Culture, Infection, Poison, or Toxin" that may have registered a negative reading on Page 1, go to Pages 2 and 3 of your Work-Lists. These have been compiled from *The Family Medical Encyclopedia.* These lists give you both a general and a specific way to check out the conditions that have been diagnosed or discovered. Further information concerning these conditions is also available under each listing. The same information can be used in conjunction with your anatomy charts to locate the problem areas.

*   *   *   *   *

Work-List Page 4

It is important to check the information on Page 4. This page concerns environmental pollution: radiation sickness and fall-out, and lists some of the main smog components; harmful metallics (traces), and poisons which may be present in food and therefore get into your body. Everyday we hear of new chemicals in our environment that are dangerous. There is room on this page (and most of the other pages) for you to add words; add any poisons that you suspect you might be exposed to at home or at work. On this same page is a complete basic mineral element list for making water and soil analyses. This is done by using the 120° line of demarcation for the pH. factor and seeing which elements are absent, which show up as being present in small quantity through negative readings, and which are present in abundance or even in excess as indicated by a positive reading. There is also a list of principal primary fission products for radiation detection work; a list or radioisotopes used in medicine. All of these can of course be correlated to the conditions present in the primary witness's body.

*   *   *   *   *

How To Neutralize Agricultural Sprays and Food Additives

It is a simple matter to find out with the pendulum that many foods are not healthy for us to eat! Many chemical sprays contain pesticides, metallics, and poisons and are being used very widely in agriculture. There are also a great many additives, such as nitrates and nitrites, that have made our food very different from what it used to be. Even seeds are sprayed before they are put on the market. We ingest all of this poison but there is something you can do about it. Clorox bleach, sea salt, and Bicarbonate of soda have been tested under laboratory conditions and proven to be successful in neutralizing radioactivity, and in oxidizing some of the harmful metallics, additives, food coloring, and smog chemicals out.[1] Seeds and food can be soaked in what is called a "Clorox bath" for 10-15 minutes. You add half a teaspoon of Clorox bleach to each gallon of water you use. Other bleaches are all right, but do not seem to have quite the same effect as Clorox. (In Europe use *Javelle Wasser* 7%.) After this Clorox bath, soak the food in fresh water for 10

44

minutes to get the odor out, then clean and store the food; you will be amazed to find that it remains fresh and crisp much longer, and will not spoil as rapidly as untreated food.

As I mentioned earlier, aluminum utensils poison the food with which they come in contact. Similarly, aluminum foil—a so-called modern miracle—is most damaging when wrapped around our food. The pendulum will easily show you the presence of a trace of aluminum in any food that has been wrapped or cooked in this dangerous material even for a very short time. The problem with aluminum is due to its very low frequency rate; any substance wrapped or cooked in aluminum is itself brought down in frequency to the same low level, which is (numerically speaking) a very negative state.

In checking your cosmetics and household products, especially deodorants (as mentioned earlier), check them also for aluminum. Do not use them, because you will absorb aluminum through the pores of your skin from an underarm deodorant, thereby causing the metallic to enter your lymph glands. Similarly, living extensively in such homes as aluminum travel trailers and mobile homes can be a very depleting situation. A little later we will learn what we can do to help clear our bodies of some of these chemicals and metallics so prevalent in our daily lives. Several different suggestions will be made for your consideration, and you can then check them out yourself against your witnesses to see if they are appropriate in your particular case.

*　*　*　*　*

Work-List Page 5 Another list which is very useful is Page 5, which is a food allergy list showing different forms and categories of all foods in their original state. This is very helpful when allergic conditions are suspected. First, check the major categories, and if you get a negative reading use the list of all foods in that category to find those which give negative readings. Make a list of these foods and keep checking them at intervals. Some readings may indicate only that a particular food is not needed by the body at that time. For instance, if you have eaten eggs for breakfast, you might get a later negative reading on them, showing merely that they would not be beneficial for you at that particular time.

As you continue to check (perhaps at different times of the day for a week or so), some of these foods will show a neutral swing, indicating that they will neither harm nor help you at that particular time. Some foods, when checked later, will give positive readings, thus showing that you are not allergic to them. If others continue to show negative readings, you can begin to suspect them. If you discontinue eating these foods with negative readings for a while, they may also show neutral or even positive readings later on, showing that you have a low tolerance for them; eat less of those foods to maintain your health. The foods that continuously give negative readings can, by this process of elimination, be shown to be probably causing the allergic reactions. Then those names (or the foods themselves, if they happen to be available), can be checked against the allergic conditions to see if they are indeed the cause of the trouble. Certain foods for which you have a low tolerance may contribute to your symptoms, but may not themselves be the primary cause of your condition. If they are not, you must of course look elsewhere, perhaps among your cosmetics, your household products, or other things within your immediate environment.

*　*　*　*　*

Listen To Your Body

I would like to draw attention to the fact that your body is constantly sending signals concerning its needs, if you will only listen! Most people have desensitized their body by eating too much food, by eating the wrong foods (such as sugar), by taking alcohol or drugs, by not getting enough sleep or sufficient care, and in many other ways. Pain is not the only indicator that something is wrong or is needed by our body. There are other feelings, some quite subtle, by means of which your body is trying to tell you something—if you would only pay attention to it! You may find out, for instance, that every morning or every evening around a certain time you feel physically exhausted. Ask yourself, what have I been doing: eating, or not eating? What does my body lack? What do I feel like doing about it? When you begin to listen to your responses, to yourself, you can gradually become more and more aware of what your body is trying to tell you, which is what really counts. Surely you are familiar with your capacity to distinguish easily what you want to eat or not eat when you are ill, and you go then by your feeling of what and how much you want. That feeling is your body trying to convey its needs to you. If you listen and eat the right food in the appropriate quantity you will aid the healing process.

When you begin to pay attention to the signals from your body (whether you are ill or not), you will find that it can tell you many things: when you are eating too much; when you crave a certain food because you really need it; how much of it you need and how often; when you are tired—not just overtired; when you need exercise or fresh air; and so on. It is because of the things you have done to abuse your body that you have dulled this innate capacity and lost a lot of your sensitive feelings. Children have much more of this innate sensitivity than adults, since they have not dulled their senses or hidden their inner feelings with a lot of ideas about things. Therefore, try to become more and more aware of what your body is telling you, and follow its indications. This will bring out your latent capacity, which will greatly help you to maintain your health. This intuition will then come to your aid in times of illness when you need it most, and you can act directly doing whatever is necessary. The same capacity will be most helpful when you search among your lists of remedies to be taken or procedures to be followed to alleviate your imbalance. In this way, you can really begin to improve the negative conditions and change your status to one of permanent good health.

*   *   *   *   *

The Two Sides of Our Being

In my own psychic research and in my work with people's psychological and physical problems, it has become very clear that the body reflects the way we live in two general ways. The left side of the body represents and registers our emotional nature, while the right side reflects our mental nature. The right side is equated with the masculine principle and the left side with the feminine. Any problem, any attitude, or any action which causes an imbalance between these two sides of our nature (namely thought and feeling), will manifest itself as a basic distortion or illness on one side. If one's decisions and actions lean heavily towards one side only, whether of thinking or feeling, an illness will occur on that side of the body. This can be a signpost to aid in the detection of the primary causes which led to the imbalance.

* * * * *

**The Principle
of Opposites**

A basic principle is involved here: nature is built of pairs of related, interacting oppositions. Sometimes extreme opposite causes produce similar symptoms, effecting the same parts of the body and causing an imbalance, although for entirely different reasons. For example, a very egotistical man, a very shy girl, or a performer with a problem with extreme stagefright, may all manifest an illness in their throat and thyroid gland, although the causes of their illness may vary remarkably due to very different emotional problems.

* * * * *

**The
Correspondence
of Action and
Emotion To
Illness**

Whatever is going on in your life, whatever you are doing, thinking, and feeling will directly affect a particular part of the body and may cause disease. It is fascinating to reflect on why a person will get a particular illness and not another, as a consequence of what is happening in his life. When the cause is discovered—through any psychological, intuitive, psychic, meditative, or practical method you are working with—it will be a major clue to aid in restoring health. Sometimes just listening to a person's expressions or his clichés will lead you directly to the "heart of the matter"—an interesting cliché in itself.

Here are some common expressions that contain direct references to parts of the body. The person using such clichés often is expressing some of the quandary he feels.
"I can't see how I":can face it
stomach it
handle it
stand it
breathe
move
take it
shoulder that responsibility
just sit still
bother to think about it.

He's: a pain in the neck
       tackling it head on
       heading for a fall
       running away from that problem.

She: blew her top
      just cracked up.

Her nose is out of joint.

I: bent over backwards
   could just die
   was all choked up.

I'm: not ready for that
      sitting around with my foot in my mouth.

My stomach turned over.

It breaks my heart.

It's beyond me.

I'll think about it tomorrow.

There are, or course, many, more sayings that show a person's emotional state of mind; I'm sure you know many yourself. It will be interesting for you to become aware of your own favorite expressions. For further information on this intrigueing subject, read *Some Unrecognized Factors in Medicine*.

Psychosomatic Correlations

It is also very interesting to note that in some cases, the illness is open for everyone to see: it is outside of the body, like a rash, a swelling, or a broken limb; in other cases it is hidden, inside the body, and private, secret, and repressed. You will soon find correlations of your own in those who flaunt their illness like a flag, and get as much psychological mileage as possible out of it. They may do this for many reasons, such as having a craving for attention, needing an excuse for what they feel is some kind of failure, or because of having a feeling of competition, etc. People often feel a need to hold on to their illness as if it were a crutch, and are afraid to let go of it.

Children's Illnesses

Such reasons are sometimes very obvious in children, who may evidence an immature jealousy, a fear of being unable to do something expected of them, or simply shyness, which makes it difficult for them to function in the harsh world with other, more aggressive children. The unfortunate and unreasonable method of teaching children by constantly comparing them with others puts great stress on them. This is a basic cause of many childhood illnesses in our fear-motivated society. If only parents and teachers would recognize what they are doing to the young with dangerous, trauma inducing competitive education and up-bringing! Fear is always crippling, and it manifests itself in a physical disability (usually affecting the urinary system), or in neurotic behavior.

¹Clark, Linda A. "Are You Radioactive?" How to Protect Yourself. Pyramid Books, 1974.

CHAPTER FOUR

Healing With the Pendulum

**How To Evaluate
What You Find**

You are now ready to take positive steps to alleviate the negative conditions that you have found. In general, there are two basically different types of negative conditions that you will encounter when searching with the pendulum. The first type involves harmful, unwanted materials in the body, such as toxins or poisons; infections, viruses, parasites, and worms; culture residues of an illness, vaccinations, medications and drugs; or food additives, pesticides and metallics; or the effects of radiation fall-out, X-ray burns, or smog. The second type of negative conditions involve predispositions, karmic or miasms; over- or under-activity of glands, functions, systems; and chronic ailments where the causes are hard to discover. The first type will, of course, affect the second type, and vice versa.

You must first get the unwanted poisons out of the body in order to free it of their effects and give it a chance to restore and balance itself. This is a major step in regaining your health, and is as important as preparing the soil before planting seeds. It has exactly the same effect, because it is much easier to regain health (and much harder for illness to take hold again) if the body is clear and free of extraneous matter.

As you begin to look for ways and means, you will find that each type of negative condition will require different remedies, and different colors. First try to remove all unwanted materials from the system, and then re-energize, rebuild, nourish, and reinstate balance to the second type of negative condition in the affected areas. After clearing the body of poisons, you will discover that there will be a separation of negative conditions into groups, each group needing similar, specific remedies, so the task of doing something will clarify itself the more you work on it.

**Health and
the Pendulum**

You can use your knowledge of the pendulum in three ways: first, to maintain your health; second, to clear the body of unwanted materials, and third, to change the underlying causes of imbalance to balance. One way to maintain your health is to check to see which vitamins, minerals, and supplements you really need on a daily basis. You might not be taking enough of some or be taking too much of others. This is not only a waste of money but places the body in the position of having to eliminate any excess. Since the pendulum can clearly tell you your own state of health, it is no longer necessary to rely on what someone else tells you or what you read. No one can know exactly what your particular needs are, what your tolerance factor is, or how well your body utilizes food. These depend on many factors that influence your biochemical make-up, such as age, sex, whether you drink alcohol, smoke, take any drugs or medication, use contraceptives, or live in a highly smog-polluted environment, etc.

The pendulum can tell you at any specific time exactly what you need. If you have some vitamins around the house, you can easily check them by holding them in your hand to see if you need them or if they are good for you.

*   *   *   *   *

**Work-List Page 6:
The First Use**

To do a more thorough job, and to know more specifically your particular needs, a complete list of all vitamins, supplements and minerals is helpful. You can go down the lists on Page 6 and establish what you really need, using only your primary witness on the determination board. A negative reading on any item indicates a deficiency. Make a secondary witness of that item and then use the list of numerical units on the same page to establish the exact amount you need a day, and how often to take it.

If you have a multiple vitamin that is good for you, which you have been taking and want to continue, place it on your primary witness (in the witness circle) and go down the list again to see what else you need. If you find a need for another item and have it around, put it in the witness circle also; continue in this manner using actual substances or their names as secondary witnesses. You can continue to check to see if you need anything more by using this accumulative method of detection. In this way you can find out exactly what you need, how often to take it, and how to divide the dosage during the day.

If you feel ill one day and wish to give your body extra nourishment, go to these same lists and see what you might do to give yourself what you need. This time, make a secondary witness specifying the illness or symptoms, so you can determine what else might be needed, in addition to the usual daily intake. For example, if you feel that you are catching a cold, you can find out how much more vitamin C you should take to counteract this condition.

* * * * *

The Use of the Remedy Lists

Work-List Page 6: Further Uses

You have just learned the first and simplest use of the remedy lists. Work-List Page 6 is a general remedy list and contains names of things to use that you will probably have around the house. You will find yourself adding your own favorites as you use this page. There is also a complete list of glandular extracts, as well as some packs to use, some applications, various heat lamps, and so on. Lists of numerical amounts in convenient categories are on all remedy lists, and you can also check how many times to take or administer a treatment, and the duration of each single treatment. Some of the items on this page are used for specific purposes, such as in first aid; for instance, cream is safe to use as an eyewash if some foreign matter is caught in your eye, and milk is used for skin rashes, burns, poison oak, or any itching. A teaspoon each of honey and apple-cider vinegar in a glass of warm water (a well-known remedy in folk medicine) is very good for stabilizing the acid-alkaline balance. This remedy is also used in folk medicine to relieve the pain of arthritis and to settle an upset stomach.

There is also a list of baths to take for various reasons. If you have metallics, pesticides, poisons, radiation, or X-ray burns in your system, you will find the different baths extremely helpful. A 'Clorox bath' will remove some of the effects of pesticides, metallics and poisons. Usually one cup of Clorox in a tub of water will oxidize some of this residue out if you soak in it 10 - 20 minutes (the same as with your food); ask your pendulum for specifics. A pound of sea salt and a pound of baking soda (Bicarbonate of soda) in a tub of water will neutralize the high acidity due to radiation and X-ray burns. An Epsom salt bath is also very effective for poisons and toxins. Many people use these baths alternately for maintaining their health in the polluted environment in which we live. Vinegar, herbs and mineral baths will also draw toxins and poisons out of the body. In cases of extreme radiation or fall-out, a mixture of 1 quart of water with 1 teaspoon each of baking soda and sea salt can be drunk to counteract the effects of radiation sickness; you can also take 3 calcium lactate tablets with each glass. Cream of Tartar is also useful in this case, as is thyme tea. Whenever you need any remedies, the pendulum will tell you all the exact specifics: how much, how long, and how often to take them.

The words herbs and homeopathic are on the general remedy lists to tell you whether or not it would be helpful to look into either one of these categories; if so, there are several pages listed under both words.

*   *   *   *   *

Work-List Pages 7, 8 and 9

This herb remedy list has over 500 herb names made up from *The Herb Book*. They are listed both numerically and alphabetically as in *The Herb Book*, so that a specific name can easily be located. By looking up either a symptom or a particular herb in the book, or using what you may have heard of read about the value of an herb, it is then easy to check it out. Often several herbs are recommended for a certain condition; you can find out which one is best by choosing the one that gives the highest positive reading. See how effective it is in treating the complaint and whether another herb should perhaps be added to it. Try for a single remedy or a combination that will give you a 360° reading, which shows that it will be 100% effective. Always ask if you should combine remedies, since it might sometimes be a mistake to do so, and could result in a loss of effectiveness. If an herb gives a positive but low reading for the condition you are trying to improve, search for another one, because the higher the reading the more effective the herb will be. Then see if you should combine it with another remedy. This method will tell you if these remedies are going to be successful and to what extent. *The Herb Book* also tells you all of the various ways in which to use herbs; this information is also listed and amounts for specifics, at the end of Page 9.

*   *   *   *   *

Work-List Pages 10, 11, 12 and 13

This homeopathic remedy list is lengthy because it has been compiled from *Homeopathic Materia Medica*, the homeopathic manual. It can be used in the same way as *The Herb Book*, by looking up symptoms or modalities. At the end of Page 13, for those unfamiliar with this type of treatment, are lists of prepared homeopathic remedies, including the twelve tissue salts—or cell salts as they are more commonly called. These cell salts are a good introduction to this whole field, since they give nourishment to the body; i.e., they nourish the cells of the body. There is a little booklet available at almost any health food store called *The Biochemic Handbook*, which explains the theory and practice of homeopathic medicine and the recommended use of these tissue salts.

Let me mention here that if you find a residue of a vaccination infection or culture still present in the system, see whether the remedy Thuja Occidentalis might be the appropriate one to take; it has been established by homeopaths to be excellent in clearing the body of vaccination residues.

Before using homeopathic remedies, please learn more about them and about the theory underlying them. Just because they are available without prescription and look very small and innocent does not mean that they should be used indiscriminately.

*   *   *   *   *

Color Healing

Without light there would not be life. Without color there is no health. Both light and color are continually being absorbed by the body. White contains all colors, while black is the absence of color. If your environment is full of bright, clear colors your energy will be high, whereas if it is dark, murky, or black your energy level will be lower. Remember this when you choose clothes, select the interior of your car, or paint your house, because we are affected very much by everything with which we come into contact.

You can actually give yourself a neurological color-stimulus treatment by looking through the flat side of a good triangular prism. This will reflect the needed pure refractions of light directly through your eyes into your nervous system. One should be outside (preferably in the sunlight) when looking through a prism. Do not look through window glass, and be sure to remove glasses or contact lenses. The primary purpose is to absorb the rays of direct sunlight refracted through the prism. Do not look directly at the sun, of course, but only at objects in the sun. You will see all of them surrounded by an aura of rainbow colors. It is the absorption of these colors by the neurons in the brain which has a therapeutic affect on the total nervous system. After about five minutes, you will notice that the colors look more brilliant and you will see some colors that you may not have noticed before. Looking through a prism is not only beneficial for color blindness and all eye problems, it will give you an immediate energy treatment. If you check your phyical energy (from your thumb reflex point, or from Page 1) before and after looking through a prism you will get an improved reading.[1]

In the same way, visualizing, meditating on, looking directly at, wearing, eating, or surrounding yourself with a needed color can greatly enhance your health and vitality. You can also treat yourself in certain specific areas of the body by visualizing color pouring into that part and alleviating the condition. Color can also be projected physically by using a lamp with color lenses.

Very recent experiments have proven that color has a definite effect on people prone to violent behavior. Positive results were immediately seen by the method of muscle testing for release of stress. Having prisoners look at large cardboards of color, or painting rooms and cells in certain colors was found to have a beneficial effect on their behavior patterns.

For these reasons, it is important to know the potential and quality of each color so one can work with them wisely, since some colors produce exactly opposite effects. Because contradictory statements have been made in the past concerning color, I did some extensive psychic investigation into the matter, and I will share some of my results here. I do not ask anyone to accept my conclusions without question; ask your pendulum to decide which color is appropriate for each need and thus rely on on one else. I feel that color has tremendous healing potential. I always search first for the proper color to use, for it is the most powerful of all remedies. Sound, which is closely aligned with color, is also a major healing energy source, but will not be discussed here as it is unavailable to most people.

*   *   *   *   *

Work-List
Page 14

I will now discuss the three primary colors, the three secondary colors, and the six intermediate colors that are named in art. No fancy descriptive names will be necessary; a color wheel from an art supply store will show you the approximate shades.

Primary colors are those from which all other colors may be derived. A secondary color is an equal mixture of two primary colors, and an intermediate color is an equal mixture of a primary and a secondary color.

Primary colors balance energy activity and should always be used first to treat the cause of the illness and restore balance. Secondary colors aid the healing process which has been set in motion and help maintain the balance. Intermediate colors refine and complete the treatment. Please note that these three steps in using colors again reaffirm the three aspects of order discussed previously. The general rule is to use pure primary colors first in treating extreme conditions, and then go to secondary and intermediate shades to finish the balancing procedure—in other words, work from negative readings up to 360°, or total balance, free from any energy distortion.

Yellow

The life force (or *prana*, as it is called in Eastern cultures) enters the etheric body through the *chakras* or energy centers, and is then distributed throughout the physical body by the glandular system. Pure yellow is male-female in quality. Yellow is the life-force, coming from the sun. It is antiseptic, and destroys any unwanted invasion or residue in the body. It functions through each cell, re-energizing and thus supporting all cell activity. I use yellow for depleted conditions, during illness and for depression, when

57

due to physical causes. Use yellow whenever energy is low and growth is required. For further details on this and all colors discussed, read the description of each on Work-List Page 14.

Red

Red is a positive color. It stimulates and brings all conditions up to normal. I use red for under-activity and any low, deficient conditions.

Blue

Blue is a negative color. It reduces and brings all conditions down to normal. I use blue for over-activity, fever, cancer, and any high, excess conditions.

Violet

Violet, which is a combination of red and blue, is an exception to the rule that one should use a primary color first. It acts most potently on the etheric body. I use violet first to reinstate balance in emergencies, in extreme conditions such as shock, or in out-of-the-body states. It is for emergency purposes only, and should later be used in its milder form, lilac. After using violet, when the emergency is over, use either red, blue, or yellow. Be careful when using violet, but do use it whenever there is a great need to balance the physical, emotional, and mental aspects of the patient.

Green

Green, which is a combination of yellow and blue, has the ability to stimulate the body's own self-healing mechanisms. I use green to aid cell growth, and to augment all healing activity. Perhaps that is why there is so much green in nature; it has the soothing potential to bring out natural tendencies for order, balance, and health.

Orange

Orange, which is a combination of yellow and red, aids the assimilation of all elements acting on or entering the body. I use orange to aid digestion, elimination, and functional disorders, and to assist other remedies being used.

The potential qualities of the intermediate colors are combinations of the primary and secondary colors and help to complete the treatment by refining what has already been done.

White

White is always safe to use, and is the most powerful of all colors. I use it, together with light in treating the energy centers of the body (the *chakras*). This will be discussed more thoroughly later.

The twelve colors and their numbers (1 to 12) are listed on Work-Page 1 for convenience.

[1]A better grade prism can be ordered from Edmunds Scientific Co., 7877 Edscorp Blvd., Barrington, NJ 08007.

CHAPTER FIVE

The Art of the Pendulum

Broadcasting

Let us now turn to the mysterious art and science of broadcasting in radiesthetic terms. It is not as yet possible to explain this phenomenon scientifically; however, it is possible to send a broadcast and let the results speak for themselves. How this works may not be clear, but that does not alter the beneficial results that are attained and attested to by empirical experience.

A broadcast uses actual physical properties and sends the essence of a color and a remedy to the primary witness: yourself or another person. Distance is no hindrance. The broadcast affects the etheric body and the vital energy field of the individual. It then enters the physical body in the same way that all light, color and vital energy does. For further reading concerning the etheric body see *The Etheric Body of Man.* It was written by Phoebe Bendit, a clairvoyant, and her husband Lawrence Bendit, an M.D. who specialized in psychiatry. They are also the authors of a previously mentioned book *Some Unrecognized Factors in Medicine.*

Broadcasting is one of the most powerful and exciting means of restoring balance in the body, one that affects not only the physical but also the mental emotional levels. A broadcast can restore equilibrium in a way that few other methods are able to do. The only other method that I have encountered that can achieve such spectacular results is spiritual healing, which can lead to instantaneous or miracle cures.

A broadcast must be very carefully prepared so that all the components are working together. It must be sent out in perfect harmony to be effective and bring order to the recipient. Since broadcasting is a very powerful tool, approach it with the greatest respect. The following account describes how it is being used at present in the United States.

When considering a broadcast, the very first thing to check is to see whether or not you should do it at all. You can send a broadcast either for a specific condition or as a general energy boost. Use your witnesses and keep in mind what you are doing for a condition, then simply point to the word "Broadcast" on your Work-List Page 1. If you get a positive reply, use the witness supplied, saying "Broadcast" or (as I will explain later), "White-Light Broadcast." Place it in the witness circle on top of the primary witness, with the name of the specific condition you wish to work on. Now you are specifically checking on and determining how to broadcast for that particular condition.

Take a sheet of paper and begin to make a broadcast chart similar to the one reproduced on the next page, Diagram 9.

Diagram 9

63

BROADCAST CHART

Witness Name

BROADCAST DATE:								
CONDITION								
COLOR NO.								
LIGHT								
WHITE LIGHT BROADCAST								
REMEDY & AMOUNT								
ANATOMY CHART NO.								
DURATION TIME								
REPEAT BROADCAST								
OTHER TREATMENTS: ORALLY, BATHS, ETC.								

Preparing a Broadcast Chart

Place the name of the person, the date, and the person's condition on top and fill in the information as you go along. Since there are so many factors involved and it is not easy to remember them all, it is simply a matter of convenience to write everything down as you discover it. This broadcast chart information can then be used like all your other lists and diagrams: it can be placed on a black paper to recheck the condition or to see if you need to repeat the process exactly or change some of it. Put the negative degree reading which is showing each time next to the name of the patient's condition. This is done so that you will be able to check for changes after the broadcast.

Which Color To Use

Your next decision involves what color to use. First check the primary colors listed on Page 6, or on Page 1, and see which one is appropriate. In later follow-up broadcasts you will find that you will have to change first to a secondary color and then to an intermediate color in order to complete the cycle of the healing process (as discussed earlier). Put the number of the color on your chart.

Which Remedy To Use

Now you can ask whether a remedy should be used and, if so, find the best one available by the method discussed earlier. This may be the same remedy you found before, or even something stronger, often one which can not be taken orally. The remedy might change in future broadcasts to something milder, often at the same time as the colors change, or it might be required in smaller amounts. When you have found the best, most appropriate remedy, make a secondary witness of it and determine the amount to use in the broadcast. Put this information on your broadcast chart as well.

Which Anatomy Chart To Use

The next thing you need to find out is which anatomy chart would be best to use. Check the names of those listed on Work-List Page 1, and pick the one with the highest positive reading. If a broadcast is to be sent to a specific part of the body, it will be easy to choose from the charts; however, to send to a system or a function, look at the artery or vein charts for more general treatment. When you have chosen the most appropriate anatomy chart in the same way, and have selected the one with the highest reading for the condition you are working on, put its number on your broadcast chart. Now, holding the pendulum over the witnesses, run your pointer over this anatomy chart and locate the exact place which requires healing; put this number or name on your broadcast chart also. If it is a specific part of the body it will be easy to locate. If it is a more general type of broadcast, the artery, vein, or digestive system charts can be used, for example, to send the healing energy through the heart, the solar plexus, or the stomach.

As mentioned before, you should have a blood-spot-witness of the person to whom you are sending the broadcast. The blood-spot will assure that the healing energy is sent not only to the person for whom it is intended, but specifically to the corresponding area or part of his body. Therefore, it will go exactly where it is intended to go, and nowhere else.

How Long To Broadcast

The next factor you must determine is how long the broadcast should last. By using the series of numerals on Work-List Page 1, or on any of the remedy list pages, you can find out how many minutes are required for a particular broadcast. The pendulum will tell you precisely how long. For instance, try pointing to 10 minutes; if the answer is yes, try 60 minutes, and if you get a no there, then go down to 30 minutes. If you get a yes again, go on up in number; if you get a no, go on further down; keep checking until you find the exact time. This is very essential because too long a broadcast time would have the same result as overdosing. Enter that information on your broadcast chart as well.

Repeating the Broadcast

The last thing you must check is whether or not to repeat the same broadcast again that same day. If not, then you can check the reults and the patient's condition the following day by going over the broadcast chart of the day before. See if a broadcast should be repeated exactly or if a change is indicated with regard to any one of the components on it. Having a carefully made-up chart in the first place makes it so much easier to keep a check on a condition from then on. If no change is indicated, you need not go through the whole procedure again. You can understand now how easy it is to forget a detail. It is essential for one to be a responsible pendulist, so keep a precise record for this very reason.

Some broadcasts are so highly effective the first time that the components will change to the second and third phase after just one broadcast each. Consequently only three broadcasts will be necessary to get the desired result. However, it is much more likely that each one will have to be repeated (depending on the gravity of the situation) before a change is indicated. The remedy might remain the same for a longer time, or possibly all the way through the series. By checking the reading of the condition with which. you are working each day, you will note the amount of change. The effects of a broadcast will take some time to enter and affect the physical body, so you can not expect to get an accurate reading immediately after sending one out. However, often a fever will go down, or a pain will sub- side or disappear altogether, during or soon after a broadcast, thus indicating that you are on the right track.

Now you can check out the remedy, by leaving all the broadcast information in the witness circle (place it on a black surface or use the name), and see if it should be used orally or in any other way, such as an application or a bath. Mark that information on your broadcast chart also.

*　　*　　*　　*　　*

How To Send a Broadcast

You are now ready to set up an actual broadcast. First place the anatomy chart you have chosen on a table made of a neutral material such as wood, glass, or plastic, with the head or top of the anatomy chart to the north. Next place the blood-spot- witness on the anatomy chart at the exact location decided upon. (You will find as you actually set up a broadcast that it is convenient to check back to the broadcast chart you just made). Next you will need the color specified. I use 4-inch-square Cathedral Glass plates; I have two of each color for use in a broadcast. You can put a primary and a secondary plate together to form an intermediate color. You will have to use the art color-wheel as a guide and go to a glass store to find the colors you need. Glass has a polarity which must be aligned with the north-south magnetic field of the earth. You can deter- mine this polarity in the glass plate by placing it on the table and holding the pendulum over it. A yes swing will show that it is pro- perly aligned with the north-south line. If rotated it will show a negative reading, if rotated twice a positive reading, and if rotated three times a negative reading again. By the positive swing you can easily establish which way the polarity runs from one edge to the opposite edge. This is the right way to place it on the blood-spot. It will be helpful to store the glass in such a manner that you need not check its polarity every time; you can do this by laying all the glass plates in the same direction, or by standing them all up the same way.

Next place an 8 oz. glass or jar on the color plate containing the amount of remedy you have already determined to be necessary, and put an ordinary 4-inch-square piece of plate glass on top of the remedy container. Now put a similar size glass container almost full of distilled water on top of that. I use distilled water to avoid any excess minerals; however, if it is not available it is not absolutely imperative. Other water, as pure or well-filtered as possible, can be substituted. Water radiates energy. Its beneficial effects are felt whenever you are near an ocean, a lake, or a river. The water will help radiate the energy from the broadcast set-up to the person on the receiving end. Now place the matching color plate of glass on top of the water container.

The final item you need is a large horseshoe magnet. I use a 16 oz. magnet which has a 50-lb. pull. A 10 or 12 oz. magnet will probably do as well. Find the positive pole by a positive swing over one end; the other end will be a negative swing. Place the magnet with the positive end to the north on top of the second colored glass plate. The opposite, negative end will point to the south.

Take a moment now to check to see if you have gotten everything correct by asking for a positive swing from the pendulum. Should it show a negative swing, you may have forgotten something; perhaps you forgot to line up one of the three glass plates or to align the magnet properly in a north-south direction; if so, you will have to go back and correct this, or the broadcast will not work. As soon as the magnet is placed on top, the broadcast starts. See Diagram 10, the Broadcast Set-Up, on the next page.

Diagram 10

BROADCAST SET-UP

68

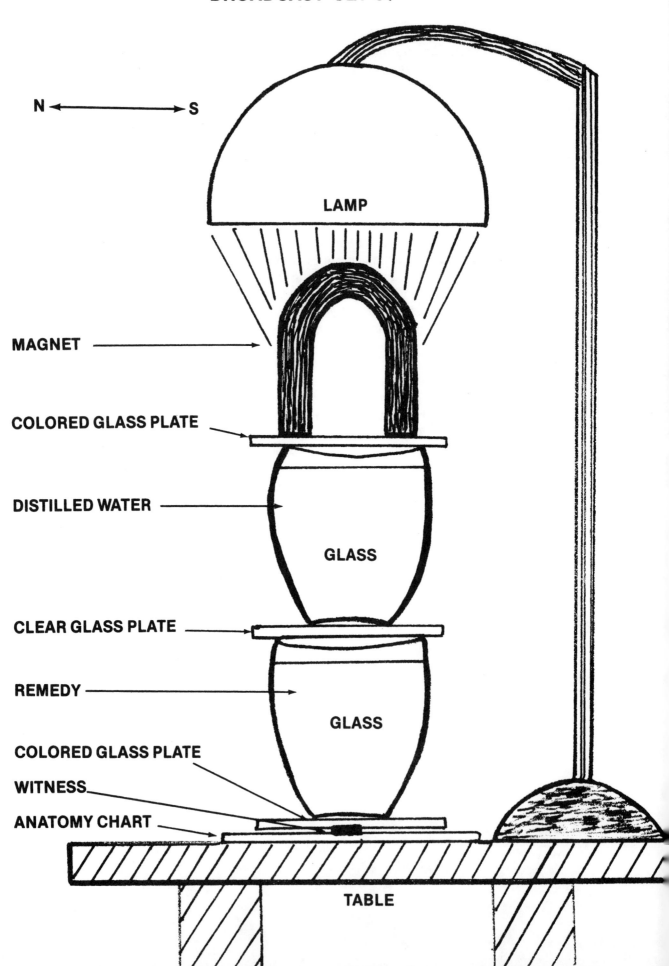

N ← → S

LAMP

MAGNET

COLORED GLASS PLATE

DISTILLED WATER

GLASS

CLEAR GLASS PLATE

REMEDY

GLASS

COLORED GLASS PLATE

WITNESS

ANATOMY CHART

TABLE

Testing the Broadcast Energy

As soon as you have completed the entire broadcast set-up, the pendulum will show you the energy radiation being sent out from it, if you test it all around the set-up. Now set a timer for the correct time needed for the broadcast and let it go. Remove the magnet as soon as the timer rings; this will stop the broadcast.

Your pendulum will now show you some interesting things. First, just before the right amount of time has elapsed, the pendulum will start swinging from the positive 'yes' swing to neutral, then go negative, back again to positive, and then stop completely. The pendulum is indicating that the broadcast is completed! If all the essence of the remedy has been sent out it will remain motionless when you check it. If there is still some essence left it will go back to a slow, rather weak, positive swing. Observe this if you like; you will find the way the pendulum seemingly wants to talk to you fascinating!

Dismantling a Broadcast

When you dismantle a broadcast set-up, you will find that the polarity in the glass plates is almost zero and you will get very little rotation from the pendulum. This must be corrected, either by washing the plates in cold water, which is a nuisance, merely by clinking them gently together, or by scraping one over the other; the sound will restore their resonance. Do this before you put them away so that they are ready for use the next time you need them. You need not check this out each time: after once testing this for yourself, just take it for granted, and get in the habit of restoring the resonance by clinking them. This alone will show you that something has happened during the broadcast, since they will usually be run down like an old battery.

If you check the essence of the remedy you have used, you will find that it may be completely depleted, producing only a neutral or very slightly positive swing; this shows that the essence has been transmitted to the patient. Sometimes a remedy can be used over again if it has enough essence remaining. Your pendulum will tell you whether you can use the remedy again; simply ask it. If it is a remedy that can be taken orally, you can of course do so as part of your daily dosage. You can also drink the water used in the broadcast—but only if the remedy used is edible—since some of the remedy's essence will remain in the water. The essence of the color used will also be in the water; by drinking it you can give yourself a color treat!

Examples of Broadcasts

Following is an example of a broadcast. For example, if you are trying to counter the effects of metallics or poisons in your body, you will probably find that they are lodged throughout the digestive tract, and are also sometimes in the muscles, joints, or in the blood. Therefore the vein chart might be very useful, and you should place the blood-spot-witness on a central area such as the solar plexus, stomach, or on a major vein. The color used will most likely be red in order to burn out the unwanted matter. The remedy might be Clorox (same as your Clorox baths mentioned earlier) or salt, soda, vinegar, Epsom salts, or some harsh agent designed to give the initial power needed to dislodge stubborn residues from the body. This type of broadcast is used to work out the first type of problem: the removal of unwanted matter. Since you can not drink Clorox, it can be used in this manner without harmful effects. After this initial broadcast, the color and remedy you need will change to something milder.

For broadcasting for the second type of condition—in which you want to nourish the body or work on basic causes—you will probably use a vitamin, mineral, supplement, herb, or homeopathic remedy, thus applying the theory that "like treats like," as in homeopathy.

*　*　*　*　*

**A New
Dimension**

I have developed some additions to the original broadcasting procedure, as a result of my own research. My dissatisfaction with certain aspects and limitations led me to do intensive psychic research to develop new methods. These additions include the use of light as a source of energy. I have found that the strength and quality of light plays an important part in the energy pattern transmitted in the broadcast. After all, spiritual healing is always done in what is known as the "White Light." My investigations resulted in my adding this fine quality of light, which I was already so familiar with in my other healing work.

When I first started working with broadcasting, I found that glands were very difficult to affect. By psychic investigations of this particular problem, I worked out a method of using light on the glandular system and obtaining much better results with all types of conditions. I found that placing a 100-watt lamp over the broadcast set-up intensified the entire broadcast, and very positive results were obtained. (It must be at least a 100-watt lamp to have the proper effect.) Therefore, always check the word "Light" on Work-List Page 1 to see if you should add it to a broadcast. It may not be indicated for the first type of condition, but it is usually extremely helpful for the second type.

*   *   *   *   *

The Chakras   The seven basic *chakras* or energy centers in the etheric body receive the *prana* and distribute it to the physical body. They are directly related and connected to seven major glands. This energy is dispersed throughout the nervous system, thereby affecting the entire body. For further information on this topic read the previously mentioned book, *The Etheric Body of Man.* Diagram 11, "The *Chakras*" and Diagram 12, "The *Chakras* and Related Material," on the next 2 pages, will clarify the position of each one of the seven major *chakras* and their relationship to the glands and the spinal chord.

Diagram 11

72

THE CHAKRAS

This shows a man, with chakras all round him.

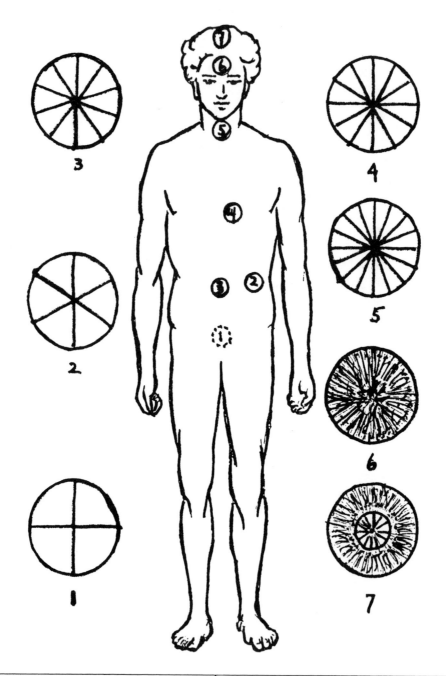

	NAME	SITUATION
1	Root Chakra	At the Base of the Spine
2	Spleen Chakra	Over the Spleen
3	Solar Plexus Chakra	Over the Solar Plexus
4	Heart Chakra	Over the Heart
5	Throat Chakra	At the Front of the Throat
6	Brow Chakra	Between the Eyebrows
7	Crown Chakra	On the Top of the Head

Diagram 12

73

THE CHAKRAS — THE GLANDS AFFECTED — SPINAL CONTACT

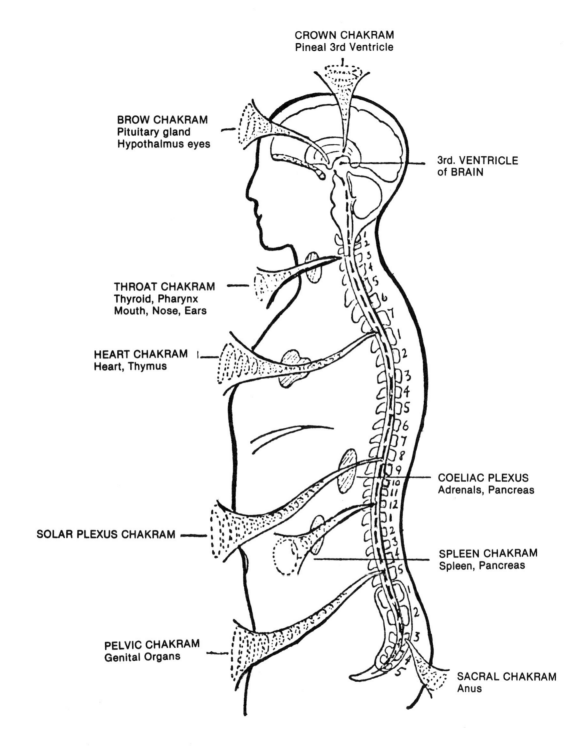

CROWN CHAKRAM
Pineal 3rd Ventricle

BROW CHAKRAM
Pituitary gland
Hypothalmus eyes

3rd. VENTRICLE
of BRAIN

THROAT CHAKRAM
Thyroid, Pharynx
Mouth, Nose, Ears

HEART CHAKRAM
Heart, Thymus

COELIAC PLEXUS
Adrenals, Pancreas

SOLAR PLEXUS CHAKRAM

SPLEEN CHAKRAM
Spleen, Pancreas

PELVIC CHAKRAM
Genital Organs

SACRAL CHAKRAM
Anus

CONDITIONS OF THE CHAKRAS

CLOSED OPENING QUICKENED RADIANT
BLENDED: SUFFICIENT INSUFFICIENT

*   *   *   *   *

**Work-List
Page 15**

The condition of each *chakra* can be checked by using the secondary witnesses supplied in the Witness Folder. Each *chakra* is associated with a specific quality of the total being. Page 15 has diagrams, information, and lists of the seven major *chakras* for work in relation to the glandular system.

*   *   *   *   *

**The White-Light
Broadcast**

In addition to the above use of light, when broadcasting to a *chakra*, I have found it to be a tremendous improvement to use white stained-glass plates and white light, instead of colored plates. This has proven to be the most efficient broadcast for improving the functions of the glands and other systems in the body. In addition, this type of "White-Light Broadcast" is highly affective in correcting shock, emotional imbalance, or unusual out-of-the-body states. If violet has been used in an emergency situation, a white-light broadcast will help to reinstate emotional balance.

For a pure white-light broadcast, the anatomy chart number 1: the "*Chakra* and Nerve Chart" must be used in order to distribute the energy throughout the entire nervous system. However, if no remedy can be found, you can put distilled water only into the bottom remedy container, as well as in the top water container. This will suffice, since the white color and light are essential healing factors in themselves. On occasion, I have used ice as a remedy in this type of broadcast in order to break a very high fever. I have also found that the pure white-light broadcast seems to balance someone's emotional nature in a way that no other remedy or drug is able to do.

**Necessity of Using
the Pendulum
Wisely**

Let me once again stress caution and careful adherence to the detailed procedures described here. Careless, half-hearted efforts in this most subtle and vital form of healing will not only fall short of beneficial results, but could be harmful. It is important to work always with the greatest integrity for the benefit of yourself or another. No license is needed for this type of healing, but one should use all of this information, with its inherent potential, wisely so as to prove the value of pendulistic work and encourage its acceptance by others.

I would like to end by wishing the very best of luck to all of those interested in the healing arts. I have done my very best to describe this form of healing so that no misunderstandings concerning the science and the art of the pendulum can arise for those who have read this book carefully. I am sure it will also be of value to those who have attended my seminars on radiesthesia and healing.

May the blessings of the healing energy of the universal intelligence guide and aid you so that you may be a worker in the light of truth.

* * * * *

PROTECTING YOURSELF FROM ENERGY DEPLETION
A Talk by Gabriele Blackburn
AUDIO CASSETTE — See Enclosed ORDER FORM

CONTACT US AT:

IDYLWILD BOOKS
P.O. BOX 246
OJAI, CA. 93024-0246

Phone: 805-646-2646
WEBSITE: **WWW.IDYLWILDBOOKS.COM**
EMAIL: light@idylwildbooks.com

BIBLIOGRAPHY

Archdale, F.A. *Elementary Radiesthesia, and the Use of the Pendulum.* The British Society of Dowsers, 1950.

Bendit, Lawrence, J. and Phoebe D. *The Etheric Body of Man: The Bridge of Consciousness.* A Quest Book—The Theosophical Publishing House, 1977.

Boericke, William. *Homeopathic Materia Medica.* Boericke & Runyon. Boericke & Taffel, Inc., 1927.

Chapman, J.B., and Perry, Edward L. *The Biochemic Handbook.* Formur, Inc., 1970.

Edmonds, H. *Some Unrecognized Factors in Medicine.* Edited by Tudor and Associates. A Quest Book—The Theosophical Publishing House, 1976.

Frohse, Franz; Brodel, Max; and Schlossberg, Leon. *Atlas of Human Anatomy.* College Outline Series. Barnes & Noble Books, 1959.

Lust, John B. *The Herb Book.* Bantam Books, 1974.

Mermet, Abbé. *Principles and Practice of Radiesthesia.* Watkins Publishers, 1935.

Reyner, J.H.; Laurence, George; and Upton, Carl. *Psionic Medicine: The Study and Treatment of Causative Factors in Illness.* Samuel Weiser, Inc., 1974.

Richards, W. Guyon. *The Chain of Life.* Leslie J. Speight Ltd., 1954.

Schifferes, Justus J. *The Family Medical Encyclopedia.* Pocket Books, 1959.

Westlake, Aubrey T. *The Pattern of Health.* Shambala, 1973.

THE SCIENCE AND ART OF THE PENDULUM:
A Complete Course in Radiesthesia

By Gabriele Blackburn

Published by:
IDYLWILD BOOKS
P.O. Box 246, Ojai, CA 93024
(805) 646-2646
e-mail: light@idylwildbooks.com

Paperback 8½ x 11
96 Pages
ISBN: 0-9613054-1-X
© IDYLWILD BOOKS 1988

Visit us at: www.idylwildbooks.com

This course emphasizes the practical use of the pendulum in maintaining a state of health by determining the underlying causes of disease. The ancient art of the pendulum, now called Radiesthesia, or Psionic healing, opens many new fields of research, and when learned correctly can be an invaluable source of self-help. The proper use of the pendulum can determine many conditions in the body which no other tests will show, for example, the amount of pollution caused by our environment. The pendulum can guide one to lessen or eliminate states of imbalance, using natural, herbal or homeopathic remedies. With Radiesthesia the pendulist can determine the need for vitamins, minerals, and supplements on a daily basis; also which remedies and dosage to use when ill.

Through the author's psychic investigations into the conditions of the etheric body, she has developed new methods of using the pendulum. Insights into the principles of healing are pointed out in diagrams and shared. In this course she teaches the meaning, potential, and varied uses of color healing. Also included is how to test and treat each of the chakras, or nerve centers, for balancing the vital energy flow. The pendulist can measure predispositions, thereby having a unique tool to maintain a state of health. The mysterious art of "Broadcasting" healing remedies is also gone into very thoroughly. This course is both for the beginner, the professional healer, and anyone who is interested in broadening their understanding of healing, and the use of the pendulum.

Gabriele Blackburn is a spiritual healer and clairvoyant. She has worked with doctors, psychologists and scientists, which together with her psychic investigations has enabled her to bring out many unique facets concerning the healing of the psychological and physical aspects of man. She always approaches her work in a creative way, which leads to many new discoveries in the area she terms, "Holistic Spiritual Healing."

Gabriele Blackburn has taught Radiesthesia and Healing seminars in the United States, Canada, New Zealand, and Europe to many health interested groups. Born in Europe, she has lived in India, and traveled extensively. She now resides in Ojai, California, and was married to the late Albert Blackburn, author of Now Consciousness and Worlds Beyond Thought.

PLEASE SEND ME:

	Each	How Many?	Amount
The Book and All Materials Listed Below:	$40.00	_____	_____
The Book Only:	$10.00	_____	_____
Author's Pendulums:	$6.00	_____	_____
Determination Boards and Pointers:	$6.00	_____	_____
1 oz. Horseshoe Magnets:	$7.00	_____	_____
Witness Folders: 50 Witnesses and Blood-Spot Envelopes:	$4.00	_____	_____
15 Work-List Pages and 18 Anatomy Charts:	$7.00	_____	_____

TOTAL ORDER:	_____
California Residents add 7% Sales Tax:	_____
U.S. Mailing and Handling $3.50:	_____
Foreign: $5.00 Surface Mail:	_____
$15.00 Air Mail:	_____
TOTAL ENCLOSED:	_____

*Send check or money order **payable on any U.S. Bank** to:*

IDYLWILD BOOKS
P.O. Box 246, Ojai, CA 93024

Order to be Sent to:

Name: _____

Address: _____

City: _____ State: _____ Zip: _____

PROTECTING YOURSELF FROM ENERGY DEPLETION:
A Talk by Gabriele Blackburn

Author of
**THE
SCIENCE
AND ART
OF THE PENDULUM:**
A Complete Course in Radiesthesia

Produced by:
IDYLWILD BOOKS
P.O. Box 246, Ojai, CA 93024
(805) 646-2646

Audio Cassette:
Time: 1 Hour
© IDYLWILD BOOKS 1986
e-mail: light@idylwildbooks.com   ~   Visit us at: www.idylwildbooks.com

---

This tape is of vital importance to anyone involved in the healing arts, or working with the sick and dying, anyone overly sensitive to people, crowds, large cities, or in constant negative relationships. In order to stay healthy it is absolutely essential to know how to protect yourself from energy depletion, which affects you physically, emotionally, and mentally. How and why you may have opened yourself up to harmful outside influences, is gone into very thoroughly, and the many different ways in which you can protect yourself are carefully explained. You will learn what you can do yourself, but when it is necessary to seek help, where to find it.

On the second side of this tape are meditation-visualizations for general and specific protections. These include protections from illness, dangerous animals, anger and violence. Different ways are shown how you can be cleansed from negativity, which is picked up so easily. Also you are taught many effective ways to protect other people, your home, car, or an object. Furthermore, you will learn how to deal positively with negative people, environments and situations. Through these creative visualizations you will be able to increase your energy level and to live a healthier, safe life.

Gabriele Blackburn is a spiritual healer and clairvoyant. She has worked with doctors, psychologists and scientists, which together with her psychic investigations has enabled her to bring out many unique facets concerning the healing of the psychological and physical aspects of man. She always approaches her work in a creative way, which leads to many new discoveries in the area she terms, "Holistic Spiritual Healing."

Gabriele Blackburn has taught Radiesthesia and Healing seminars in the United States, Canada, New Zealand, and Europe to many health interested groups. Born in Europe, she has lived in India, and traveled extensively. She now resides in Ojai, California, and was married to the late Albert Blackburn, author of Now Consciousness and Worlds Beyond Thought.12.5

- -

PLEASE SEND ME:

Amount

PROTECTING YOURSELF FROM ENERGY DEPLETION

*ALL TAPES
WARRANTED
AGAINST
DEFECTS*

Send check or money order **payable on any U.S. Bank** *to:*
IDYLWILD BOOKS
P.O. Box 246, Ojai, CA 93024

How Many?_____@ $6.00 each: _____
California Residents add 7% Sales Tax: _____
U.S. Mailing and Handling $3.50: _____
Foreign: $5.00 Surface Mail: _____
$15.00 Air Mail: _____
TOTAL ENCLOSED: _____

Order to be Sent to:

Name: _____

Address: _____

City: _____ State: _____ Zip: _____

THE LIGHT OF KRISHNAMURTI

· · · Gabriele Blackburn · · ·

Published by:
IDYLWILD BOOKS
P.O. Box 246, Ojai, CA 93024
(805) 646-2646
www.idylwildbooks.com   e-mail: light@idylwildbooks.com

Paperback 5⅜ x 8⅜
256 Pages
ISBN: 0-9613054-4-4
Price: $14.00
© IDYLWILD BOOKS 1996

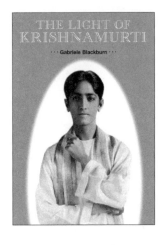

The Light of Krishnamurti relates the many-faceted mystical and spiritual occurrences of J. Krishnamurti as experienced by Gabriele Blackburn.

This is the story of the author's life in relationship to these events, their extraordinary meaning, and the profound effect they had on her. In a simple, direct, factual manner, she tells how his friendship, personal interviews, and the understanding of his teachings, helped her to resolve a life crisis, and discover an insightful way of living.

This book voices the quality of the clear Light of truth which casts no shadow. It is a personal testimony to the sacred life and teachings of Krishnamurti, that Gold Light of eternity.

Gabriele Blackburn is a spiritual healer and clairvoyant. She has worked with doctors, psychologists and scientists, which together with her psychic investigations has enabled her to bring out many unique facets concerning the healing of the psychological and physical aspects of man. She always approaches her work in a creative way, which leads to many new discoveries in the area she terms, "Holistic Spiritual Healing."

Gabriele Blackburn is the author of The Science and Art of the Pendulum, and has taught Radiesthesia and Healing seminars in the United States, Canada, New Zealand, and Europe to many health interested groups. Born in Europe, she has lived in India, and traveled extensively. She now resides in Ojai, California, and was married to the late Albert Blackburn, author of Now Consciousness and Worlds Beyond Thought.

PLEASE SEND ME: THE LIGHT OF KRISHNAMURTI

Amount

Sorry - no phone orders.

Send check or money order
payable on any U.S. Bank to:

IDYLWILD BOOKS
P.O. Box 246, Ojai, CA 93024

How Many?_____ @ $14.00 each: _____
California Residents add 7% Sales Tax: _____
U.S. Mailing and Handling $3.50: _____
Foreign: $5.00 Surface Mail: _____
$15.00 Air Mail: _____
Total Enclosed: _____

Order to be Sent to:

Name: _____

Address: _____

City: _____ State: _____ Zip: _____

SONGS OF LIGHT

Five Original Songs

Created in moments of intuition and sung

by

Gabriele Blackburn

As If With You
Keep Moving
Stupid Old Me
Thinking Of You
Meditation Is To See

AUDIO CASSETTE   20 Minutes

$5.00

PLEASE SEND ME:

SONGS OF LIGHT

ALL TAPES
WARRANTED
AGAINST
DEFECTS

Order to be Sent to:

	Amount
How Many?_____ @ $5.00 each:	_____
California Residents add 7% Sales Tax:	_____
U.S. Mailing and Handling $3.50:	_____
Foreign: $5.00 Surface Mail:	_____
$15.00 Air Mail:	_____
TOTAL ENCLOSED:	_____

Send check or money order **payable on any U.S. Bank** *to:*
IDYLWILD BOOKS
P.O. Box 246, Ojai, CA 93024

Name: _____

Address: _____

City: _____ State: _____ Zip: _____

NOW CONSCIOUSNESS:
Exploring the World Beyond Thought
By Albert Blackburn

Published by:
IDYLWILD BOOKS
P.O. Box 246, Ojai, CA 93024
(805) 646-2646
e-mail: light@idylwildbooks.com

Paperback 5³/₈ x 8³/₈
176 Pages
ISBN: 0-9613054-0-1
© IDYLWILD BOOKS 1983
Visit us at: www.idylwildbooks.com

The intimate contemporary account of one man's quest is a valuable step-by-step approach that anyone can follow on the path of self-knowledge. During an interview with J. Krishnamurti in 1944 the author underwent a radical inner transformation, a turning about at the deepest seat of consciousness. The result: Now Consciousness, the perception of reality moment-to-moment, free of time and discrimination. This awareness leads to an inner clarity that enables the individual to objectively watch the intricacies of the thought process and explore the secrets of consciousness.

Albert Blackburn's straightforward accounting of his own experiences make this work ideal for anyone interested in the dynamics of consciousness and the psychology of transpersonal experiencing. The author disputes the necessity of a linear approach to enlightenment; instead he suggests the possibility of a vertical, instantaneous breakthrough, free of time.

Albert Blackburn was born in Cincinnati, Ohio in 1910. He began a career in aviation in 1928 after graduating from the first approved flying school in the U.S. This led to barnstorming, flight instruction, and eventually to airport ownership and flight school operations from 1938 to 1950. Wishing to give all of his time to his inward exploration of consciousness, he gave up his airport business and moved to Ojai, California. Mr. Blackburn was a member of the Theosophical Society from 1934 to 1944, was associated with the Happy Valley School from 1948 to 1958, and Krishnamurti Writings Inc. from 1946 to 1966; he was also briefly associated with the Krishnamurti Foundation of America. Since 1974 he has been teaching, writing, and giving talks in various places in the U.S. and Canada, utilizing his own experiences and understanding of life.

Now Consciousness: *Exploring the World Beyond Thought is a stimulating and perceptive account of Albert Blackburn's/the author's experience in transpersonal realms. The personal account of his time with Krishnamurti is especially interesting, and his treatment of the process of self-realization is – to use a word the author may regard as inappropriate – thoughtful.*

John White
Author of *"Frontiers of Consciousness"*

- -

Amount

PLEASE SEND ME: **NOW CONSCIOUSNESS**

How Many?_____ @ $8.95 each: _____
California Residents add 7% Sales Tax: _____
U.S. Mailing and Handling $3.50: _____
Foreign: $5.00 Surface Mail: _____
$15.00 Air Mail: _____
TOTAL ENCLOSED: _____

Send check or money order **payable on any U.S. Bank** *to:*
IDYLWILD BOOKS
P.O. Box 246, Ojai, CA 93024

Order to be Sent to:

Name: _____

Address: _____

City: _____ State: _____ Zip: _____

FURTHER EXPLORATION INTO NOW CONSCIOUSNESS:
Discussions with Albert Blackburn
Author of **NOW CONSCIOUSNESS**

Produced by:
IDYLWILD BOOKS
P.O. Box 246, Ojai, CA 93024
(805) 646-2646
e-mail: light@idylwildbooks.com

Audio Cassette:
Time: 1 Hour each
© IDYLWILD BOOKS 1986
Visit us at: www.idylwildbooks.com

We invite you to participate in this exciting exploration into the world beyond thought. In these tapes Albert Blackburn, with his wife Gabriele, discuss his creative and completely extemporaneous, step-by-step exploration into insight. Using the words as a mirror, the listener can be led imperceptibly into an actual experiencing of what is being discussed. True listening, in which there is no judgment, evaluation or a retreat into a preconceived idea, invites holistic understanding at the level where inner transformation can occur.

#1 An Introduction to Now Consciousness
Covers: A comparison between occultism, mysticism and now consciousness. Do all paths lead to the ultimate Truth? Experiencing reality beyond psychological time. The results of 'meditation.' What is a religious life?

#2 Direct Perception
Covers: The ending of psychological time. The possible effect of computerized living on brain development. The possibility of by-passing conditioning through direct perception.

#3 Experiencing
Covers: The fundamental difference between an experience and experiencing. How experiences are routed through the brain into the content of consciousness. Experiencing the completeness of each moment opens the door to insight and self-discovery. With insight we can live intelligently.

#4 The Quiet Mind
Covers: Can the manipulation of thought, through meditation lead to a quiet mind? What is real stillness? How true stillness can come into being with no effort. The ending of the psychological 'me,' and the discovery of reality moment-to-moment.

#5 Exploring the World Beyond Thought
Covers: What is the origin of thinking? Two kinds of memory. Insight – direct action – faith. The difference between knowledge and knowing. Can one live without psychological time?

#6 Enlightenment
Covers: The real meaning and results of enlightenment: freedom from the known, use of a different energy, no conflict, no fear, order, integrity, understanding, faith, harmlessness, honesty and inner peace.

#7 Holistic Understanding
Covers: Four levels of understanding. Integrated understanding on all levels is the beginning of an entirely new way of living. Is suffering an intrinsic part of the evolutionary process? How to completely eliminate psychological suffering. What is spiritual alchemy?

		Each	How Many?	Amount
PLEASE SEND ME:	#1 **Introduction to Now Consciousness**	$6.00	_____	_____
	#2 **Direct Perception**	$6.00	_____	_____
All tapes	#3 **Experiencing**	$6.00	_____	_____
warranted	#4 **The Quiet Mind**	$6.00	_____	_____
against	#5 **Exploring the World Beyond Thought**	$6.00	_____	_____
defects	#6 **Enlightenment**	$6.00	_____	_____
	#7 **Holistic Understanding**	$6.00	_____	_____

TOTAL ORDER: _____
California Residents add 7% Sales Tax: _____
U.S. Mailing and Handling $3.50: _____
Foreign: $5.00 Surface Mail: _____
$15.00 Air Mail: _____
TOTAL ENCLOSED: _____

Send check or money order **payable on any U.S. Bank** *to:*
IDYLWILD BOOKS
P.O. Box 246, Ojai, CA 93024

Order to be Sent to:

Name: _____

Address: _____

City: _____ State: _____ Zip: _____

WORLDS BEYOND THOUGHT:

Conversations on Now Consciousness

By Albert Blackburn

Published by:
IDYLWILD BOOKS
P.O. Box 246, Ojai, CA 93024
(805) 646-2646
e-mail: light@idylwildbooks.com

Paperback $5^{3}/_{8}$ x $8^{3}/_{8}$
218 Pages
ISBN: 0-9613054-3-6
© IDYLWILD BOOKS 1988
Visit us at: www.idylwildbooks.com

In *WORLDS BEYOND THOUGHT* Albert Blackburn guides the reader to an understanding of what it means to live moment by moment, free of the insidious thought process that causes all of our psychological problems. He emphasizes the importance of a complete awareness of the present moment, a holistic perception that can bring about a quiet mind, clarity, and order in one's life, and lead to an experiencing of that which is beyond human consciousness, which is sacred, all Love and Light.

The seven conversations that comprise the major part of *WORLDS BEYOND THOUGHT* are revised and expanded versions of actual dialogues between Albert Blackburn and his wife, Gabriele. Before his death in June, 1987, he spent months carefully editing the transcripts of these conversations, expanding and clarifying his ideas, and making certain that necessary changes did not modify or distort his meaning in any way. These thoughtful elucidations make *WORLDS BEYOND THOUGHT* a valuable study in self-realization, and the author's revolutionary insights may help others to resolve their own fundamental problems. Some of Mr. Blackburn's letters, which he felt contained a unique approach to discovering answers to the many basic questions of life, have been included with the dialogues to give the book an additional dimension.

Albert Blackburn was a close friend of J. Krishnamurti, whose teachings inspired the radical inner transformation that the author described in his previous book, NOW CONSCIOUSNESS. *Mr. Blackburn lived his life with great intensity, motivated solely by the desire to be totally free of ego, self-will, and need for personal gratification. His serious investigations into the meaning of life were expressed with a clarity that characterized everything that he wrote or spoke, every word of which originated in his own holistic understanding of life. His inner commitment brought him into extensive contact with people from many countries and many walks of life, all of whom were enriched by the deep insights that characterized his approach to living.*

Create-Your-Own
Perpetual Calendar®

Easy to use — Never out of date

∙∙
Use 12 of your own photos or pictures
∙∙

Create a treasured keepsake – a unique gift

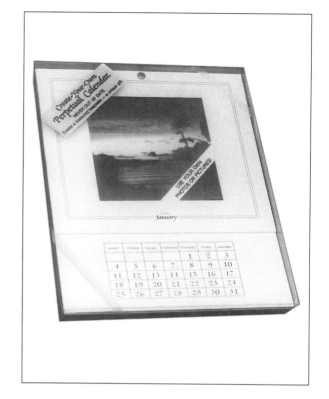

> ### ═══ A WALL HANGING CALENDAR ═══
>
> By simply using appropriate month & date cards,
> this perpetual calendar will never be out of date.
>
> Will fit standard 8 x 10 or 10 x 12 frame

AN EXCITING NEW IDEA IN CALENDARS!

ARTISTICALLY PRODUCED!!

A UNIQUE CONVERSATION PIECE!!!

You'll Love It!!!

...blished by:
...YLWILD BOOKS
...O. Box 246, Ojai, CA 93024
...05) 646-2646
e-mail: light@idylwildbooks.com
Visit us at: www.idylwildbooks.com

Month & Date Cards
Size: 8 x 10
Packaged in See-Thru Boxes
ISBN: 0 9613054-2-0
© IDYLWILD BOOKS 1986

- -

Please send me: Create-Your-Own
Perpetual Calendar®

	Amount
How Many?_____ @ $9.00 each:	_____
California Residents add 7% Sales Tax:	_____
U.S. Mailing and Handling $3.50:	_____
Foreign: $5.00 Surface Mail:	_____
$15.00 Air Mail:	_____
TOTAL ENCLOSED:	_____

> *Send check or money order*
> **payable on any U.S. Bank** *to:*
> IDYLWILD BOOKS
> P.O. Box 246, Ojai, CA 93024

Order to be Sent to:

Name: _____

Address: _____

City: _____ State: _____ Zip: _____